CUSTOMER FIRST

Create More Impact and Income
With Your Network Marketing Business

(Without Being High-Pressure or "Salesy")

Tasha Smith

Table of Contents

INTRODUCTION

Does something feel a little "off" with your network marketing business? Like you are doing everything you are "supposed" to be doing, but it's just not working how it "should," for some reason?

If so, you aren't alone.

This morning I was chatting with a successful but frustrated network marketing leader.

She shared: "I'm just supposed to keep sending these messages on social media, hoping someone will respond. I don't even know these people I am reaching out to...I wish I could connect with people and they would see what I am offering as valuable, instead of me just sitting here thinking 'OMG, nobody liked those messages.'"

This leader went on. "For me, what is hard as a leader is confidence. When I'm not getting results, how can I lead others? If what I'm doing isn't working, how am I supposed to teach my team members to run a successful business? The strategy that keeps getting pushed on us is to just keep inviting more people...and eventually you will reach a 'yes.' It isn't working.

"All I want is to be successful and for my team to feel successful, even if everyone is just earning a few hundred dollars."

Can you relate to this leader?

Over the past four years, I have asked thousands of network marketers at all levels this question, "What's hard for you?"

The answers are the same over and over again:

- I don't want to be high-pressure and pushy
- I don't know what to say when I follow-up

- I don't know what to do when someone says "yes." What do I do with them next?

- Am I good enough to be a leader?

- I don't know how to help my team be more successful

Frustration, analysis paralysis, and every day wondering, "what is wrong with ME?" have become the normal state of existence.

If you have been feeling this way too, then I want to address this.

NOTHING is wrong with you.

In fact, that is the wrong question to be asking. In the pursuit of freedom, rank goals, and a network marketing version of keeping up with the Joneses, leaders have forgotten the point of it all. Income goes up and down. Leaders are not "feeling" successful, so they stop recruiting, and the team starts shrinking.

The right question to ask is, "how do I help as many customers as possible?"

We need to get back to the basics of business.

> *"The purpose of business is to create and keep a customer."*
> **—Peter Drucker**

The solution is to take the focus off ourselves and our insecurities about being in "sales" and put the focus on the customer. We need to put the customer first.

So how do we do this?

First, we need to come to grips with the fact that you, my friend, are in sales. Your team is also in sales. This makes you a sales manager. Being in sales is not something to deny—it's something to be proud of. When we understand that we are in fact in a sales business and the job is to serve customers well, we can focus on what they want and need, and focus on impacting them positively.

The right question to ask is, "how do I help as many customers as possible?"

Second, we need to create conversations that focus on building trust, listening to customer needs, and solving their problems in the simplest way possible. We need to stop taking shortcuts in our communication with customers and spend a little more time adding value to their lives. I'm sure you have found that, oftentimes, the shortcut is actually the long way.

Third, we need to lead our teams in a way so that THEY also have a "customer first" mentality. We need to create a vision that celebrates customers AND business builders. We need to make it easy for them to improve their skills, and we need to lead by example.

Fourth, we need to rise above our insecurities that keep us from being the best version of ourselves. Once we understand these insecurities better, it is easier to overcome them.

Take a Deep Breath, I Got You

This book is going to show you that you CAN and WILL positively impact a lot of people through the sale of your amazing products.

This book is going to show you how to be more professional, be more authentic, and make sales WITHOUT being pushy, salesy, or having to follow up indefinitely.

This book is going to show you how to LEAD your team to create and serve customers well, even if they have never sold anything before.

This book is going to address the major mental roadblocks that our EGO gives us to sabotage our success. We are going to kick ego to the curb and put the CUSTOMER FIRST.

We are going to do all of this WITHOUT the choice weapon of the self-help industry: shame that you can't manifest your success. I don't know about you, but I am sick and tired of people telling you that your problem is you. It's time for some real and honest business training.

We are going to talk about what it means to love customers, the intention behind our activities, why customers act the way they do, and why you act the way you do. **We are going to use weapons like TRUTH, SKILL, and ENCOURAGEMENT to remind you that yes, you can do this.**

Are you with me? (The crowd cheers!)

At the time I am writing this intro, my team and I have trained and coached over 8,000 network marketers on sales, recruiting, leadership, and social media.

We have had clients make their first $1,000 and clients who have reached the 6-figure income level. Additionally, we have consulted with million-dollar earners to assist them in developing their training and leadership programs.

That's crazy right? Sometimes I don't even believe it. You might be wondering, "how is it that you help clients get such amazing results?"

You will get amazing results because I am not your upline trying to get you to make more sales, or trying to teach you "what I did." I am your customer, experiencing you and your company at the point of sale.

I am BEGGING YOU: "Please make it easier to buy. Please listen to me. Please care about my life. Please make it simple for me, I'm overwhelmed by all the things. Please show up for me."

If you believe in the life-changing properties of your product, you have a moral and ethical obligation to sell well. If you don't learn how to sell well, then I, your customer, am screwed.

We need to be better at helping customers get what they need if we want to change people's lives. We need to change a lot of other people's lives in order to change ours.

As you continue to read, I want to challenge you to think differently.

See through the eyes of someone who goes to bed praying for the health of their families. Imagine praying to be able to pay for all the things their family needs. Imagine them praying for the solutions that your product provides.

I want you to see through the eyes of someone willing to exchange solutions to those problems for money. That's it. It's that simple.

But I know, you are "not a salesperson." It's ok, I wasn't either. I promise, you will be the opposite of all the pushy and annoying people that are popping into your mind.

I am NEVER going to ask you to do or say anything that you wouldn't be able to say to your best friend, sister, or mom. Remember, I represent your CUSTOMER.

Together we can build up a team of "good humans" who create amazing customer experiences, and who lead and train their teams to do the same.

Imagine them praying for the solutions that your product provides.

When you finish this book, you are going to have more confidence, more motivation, more sales, greater duplication and more joy in your business.

There are a lot of people out there waiting for you to show up as your best self. There are a lot of people out there suffering without your products. I know, I was one of them.

The best day to plant a bamboo tree was 25 years ago. The second-best time is today. Likewise, since time machines don't exist, the best time to move forward is today.

Turn the page to start your journey to become a "customer first" network marketer.

SECTION 1

CUSTOMER FIRST PHILOSOPHIES

CHAPTER 1

WHY WE HATE SALESPEOPLE

Maybe I'm the only one whose Mom isn't exactly "pro-sales."

When I started my direct sales career, I had one noticeable no-sale in my first weekend: my mom. The worst part was that she had bought some of the products from another kid, but not me!

Let's fast forward a few weeks. I came home with some outlines. "Mom, I want to practice handling objections, will you practice with me?" I thought this was a slam dunk because my mom is literally the most supportive person ever.

Instead of jumping up and down with glee about how motivated her daughter was, she responded, "I hate salespeople" and walked away. UGH.

Once again, history repeated itself and I didn't listen to my mom. In a few months I was able to master, with a smile: "If I could wave a magic wand and you could afford this set of knives, which one would you prefer?" It's really quite a great line when I think back. I might need to start using that one again.

A few weeks later I mentored my first new trainee and decided I wanted to keep going in my direct sales career instead of law school. Oops.

Don't worry, there is a happy ending. My mom has realized I wasn't that "salesperson" that she hated. There were other reasons for her to be annoyed with me, but this wasn't one of them. She has since done some amazing mom things like helping me paint my offices. Each time I failed, she lovingly pointed out all of the lessons I was learning.

Several years ago, she and my step dad started an importing business. They had beautiful products, and guess who they called to help with the expo? That "salesperson."

It only took me 10 years for my mom to ask me for sales advice. Now she brags about how good I am, especially when she saw me rock her expo booth.

Why did she come around?

Because I was NOTHING like "that salesperson" she hated. I showed her at that expo that sales is about caring about people, being nice, and offering an invitation for them to move forward.

We find a problem, solve it, and then get paid. My mom has watched me do that for the past 19 years.

When you work with a highly skilled salesperson, it's a pleasure because they listen and serve you well.

I have worked pretty hard to be the kind of person that my mom would be proud of.

Are you proud of having a career in sales? If your answer isn't a resounding YES, then we need a little straight talk. We need to address our issues with "sales." This is a critical part of being successful in network marketing because you need to be proud of what you do. As much as you might want to focus on business builders, your income is going to be a reflection of how many CUSTOMERS you and your builders create. And your income, joy, and impact will be capped at your level of belief in your product, your business, and your profession.

This belief starts with an understanding of WHY people (maybe even including you) have an aversion to people in sales. Once you feel more comfortable about the truth that "sales" is not a bad word, you can move forward and focus on making a difference.

Reason #1 That We Hate Salespeople: False Stereotypes

Most people cringe when they hear the word "sales" or "salesperson." Have you ever said to yourself, or others: "I am NOT a salesperson?"

Let's list the images we think of when the word "sales" comes up:

- Cars

- Suits

- Aggressive

- Pushy

- Inauthentic

We have this image in our mind about the "car salesman" that we talked about earlier. Our culture has ingrained a stereotype in our mind that "selling" is pushy, outrageous, selfish and probably unethical.

But truthfully, sales is simply exchanging money for a product or service. There is nothing pushy, outrageous, selfish or unethical about it. It's a PROCESS that is the problem, not the selling itself.

The stereotypes about salespeople operate much like all other stereotypes we see in the world. I'm Indian, so I'll use an Indian stereotype as an example. I'll use a positive one in this example, even though the sales stereotype is a negative one.

One Indian stereotype is that we are "good at math." Indians grow up believing we are good at math. Since we are good, we like it. Since we like it, our parents buy us workbooks to do extra math. Since we have extra workbooks and lots of encouragement, we do better, further reinforcing the stereotype.

How does this apply to sales? The stereotype is that the people in sales only care about themselves. Then they believe that because they are in sales, they must care about themselves. They set goals that are primarily based on their own interests, and set up strategies that serve their own goals. They talk about these goals and these strategies, thus further reinforcing the stereotype.

What is true?

77% of the network marketing profession is women. The image of a man in a suit is simply archaic, and doesn't belong in the 21st century.

1 in 9 Americans is in some sort of sales role (including entrepreneurship), and many of them are not selling cars. That is 11% of your friends and family.

Reason #2 That We Hate Salespeople: Hollywood Portrayals

I grew up in sales before I knew anything about anything. I didn't ever know that "closing" is supposed to be gross or icky. For those of you new to sales, "the close" is the ending of a sales conversation, where a customer agrees to buy or not. "Closing the sale" often means getting that customer through the final process and to a yes decision, with money in hand.

"Closing percentage" is the percentage of sales out of the number of appointments you have completed. I thought closing was cool and helpful for much of my career.

And then I saw *Glengarry Glen Ross*. If you haven't seen it, this is an iconic film in which Alec Baldwin stars as the lead who is a "motivational trainer" for a real estate sales team. Below are some of the phrases from his most famous speech in the film.

> Baldwin pointing to a chalkboard, "ABC. A always. B be. C closing. Always be closing. Always be closing..."
>
> "You close or you hit the bricks..."
>
> "They're sitting out there waiting to give you their money. Are you gonna take it? Are you man enough to take it?"
>
> "You want to go out on those sits tonight and close, CLOSE."

It's intense. These scenes are entertaining and contain amazing acting. However, I believe it has deeply influenced the inappropriate behavior of many in the industry.

Most importantly, there is one irreconcilable problem with this scene. It's not true.

This scene portrays the salesperson in a role where he has to sell or die. It shows this idea that "closing" is something you do TO someone. A lot of people believe closing is forcing someone to do something they don't want to do. It's actually the opposite.

Some people are attracted to the *Glengarry Glen Ross* sales philosophy. They are driven by greed, unlimited income, and status. They are 100% driven by EGO. They are NOT good humans. They do want to make the sales and don't care about the people. It really stinks. This is more because of the fact that, at the end of the day, the sales industry is comprised of human beings.

You will find good humans and bad humans in any industry. There are teachers who are amazing, and there are teachers waiting to retire, doing the minimum amount of work to get by. There are honest business people, and dishonest ones.

The challenge with the bad human salespeople is that they typically are the loudest. And so "sales" feels like a bad profession, and this impacts the confidence of many network marketers.

There is a BIG difference between "customer first" sales people and "ego first sales people." They are NOT even in the same game.

What is true?

In Secrets to Closing the Sale, Zig Ziglar (a real motivational sales trainer, not an actor) says, "Closing is not something you do TO someone, it's something you do FOR someone."

> *"Closing is not something you do TO someone, it's something you do FOR someone."*

There are many definitions of the verb "close" in the dictionary. Not all of them apply, but none of them are high pressure or pushy.

My favorite definition shared on dictionary.com is: "to come together; unite."

16

I disagree with Alec Baldwin's perspective on motivating salespeople (it's ok, since the character is fictional) but I agree with one statement. We do need to "always be closing" IF we use the definition above.

Every step of the sales process needs to bring you and the customer together on the same page. Every step needs to unite their problems to your solution.

When we look at closing in this way, it changes everything. We can gain agreement at every turn. We can be kind, gracious, and compassionate, to our customers and ourselves.

The "closing of the sale" is the ending. It's the place where customers decide yes, no, or maybe. However, the "uniting" of the customer and product starts much earlier than that.

Reason #3 That We Hate Salespeople: Incomplete Training

Unethical, uncaring salespeople are not typically the reason that experiences may feel high pressure or pushy. I believe that most people aren't like that. In 19 years of sales and sales leadership experience I have come across very few people who didn't care about people and wanted to make the sale regardless.

Many of these so-called "salesy" people simply don't know better. They don't know the details of how to communicate in a way that truly conveys what they are trying to say. They don't know how to simply "acknowledge the awkward" in various situations. They don't even know they have the permission to do so.

Many people don't know the difference between a real "get to know you" question and one that feels like an interrogation. So they mean well, but end up coming across inauthentic or untrustworthy.

Just like any profession, there are nuances that sometimes don't matter, but sometimes REALLY DO.

Many brilliant trainers or leaders focus on activity instead of communication skills. Many leaders advanced to their rank or leadership role because they came with good communication skills. They wrongly assume everyone has similar skills. These leaders are "unconsciously competent." Unconsciously competent means "they don't know what they know." The training gets boiled down to "tell your story and follow-up." There are just a few missing pieces in what they are actually doing in practice. This book will fill in the blanks for you.

What is true?

Have you ever worked with a really good salesperson? How do you feel? Cared for? Listened to? Like the purchase was your idea? Well-informed but not confused?

What is the difference?

> *Well-trained individuals in sales make the process enjoyable for everyone involved.*

Well-trained individuals in sales make the process enjoyable for everyone involved. Customers trust them. They know how to listen well and ask thought-provoking questions. They care about people having a better life, and genuinely believe that their product will help those people achieve that goal. Well-trained salespeople know the right amount of information to not overwhelm the customer, and can explain it to them simply. They make the buying process quick and painless.

Reason #4 That We Hate Salespeople: Fear of Being "Salesy" Actually Creates "Salesy" Behavior

Take the first few reasons and it's easy to see why many network marketers run as far away from anything associated with "sales" as possible. In fact, I'm surprised you are even reading this book. (But thank you! Please keep reading!)

We hear terms like "overcoming objections." The thought of telling a person "don't worry, it's only a coffee a day" makes us want to cringe.

And what about following up? How many times has it been suggested to you to follow up with people? Five times? Seven times? As many times as it takes?

And so you say, "NOPE! I'm not a salesperson" and the last thing you would do is engage in sales training. You might think that if you go to sales training, they will actually train you to be like that gross and pushy person you detest.

If you don't go to sales training, you go to mindset training instead. Mindset shifting is definitely important. Our mind is often our worst enemy. However, if you have never been trained in high quality sales, and you are trying to feed your family through the sales of your product and your team sales, we have a problem. What are you left with if you don't have sales training?

You are left with telling your story and following up. On the surface, this seems like a "can't lose" strategy. It seems to work for the most successful people you know in the industry.

However, many people are actually super uncomfortable talking about themselves and following up until someone buys or dies. It's almost like the story and follow-up approach is more salesy than anything taught in actual sales training.

In an effort to not be "that person," many people inadvertently become "that person."

What is true?

The difference between a "salesy" and an "authentic" salesperson is twofold.

The first difference is the sales process. The sales process must be designed with the CUSTOMER in mind, not simply "the way my upline does it." The intention of the sales process is to focus on the most efficient and effective way to help customers solve their problems as quickly and thoroughly as possible. Period.

The second difference is the intention of the salesperson. If I am calling you only because my numbers are low, you can tell. If I am calling you because I care, you can tell. The words might be the same. The outcome might be the same. As Carl W. Buehner has said, "They may forget what you said, but they will never forget how you made them feel."

I know you are a good person, so all we need to do is add some really simple skills to that really big heart.

Customer First Takeaways

- The "car salesman" image is as outdated as the image of the woman standing in the kitchen, barefoot and pregnant, waiting for her husband to come home and read a printed newspaper.
- "Customer first" people and ego-first people are very different.
- Being in sales DOES NOT mean you are inherently ego driven, even if you like nice things.

Focusing on increasing your communication skills and using a clear "customer first" sales process will ensure that you aren't "salesy".

CHAPTER 2

WHAT DOES IT MEAN TO BE CUSTOMER FIRST?

"Customer First" is not a pecking order in your business—it's a way of life. It's taking a step back, looking into our business, and thinking about things through the perspective of the customer. We need to take off our network marketing hats and put on our customer's hat so we can see things from their eyes.

I have had many good experiences with "customer first" network marketers and LOVE the high-quality products. My bank account and a whole shelf in my pantry will serve as evidence. However, I am going to share some interactions that are not "customer first" because they illustrate how quickly customers can be turned off.

Situation #1: The Friend Request

This is an actual exchange I had with someone on Facebook. I didn't know her at all. We had one mutual friend, a guy I used to work with that I hadn't talked to in years.

L4Evah: *sends friend request

Me: Hi Dani, thank you for the friend request. It's nice to meet you. I love your Wonder Woman cover photo. :)

L4Evah: Hi Doll!! Great to meet you too!! Yes WW is the bomb!! Happy 4th! Any fun plans with the fam today!?!

Me: We had a good day swimming and spending time with family that was in town. Thanks for asking. ☺

L4Evah: Yayay!! That sounds amazing!! We pretty much did the same yayay!!

L4Evah: Soooo I'm dying to know have you evah tried [product name here]?!

Me: Thanks for asking, but I'm not interested in getting a different [product type].

L4Evah: Ok cool! What do you currently use!?

Me: [Network marketing company I already buy from]

L4Evah: Ooo thats a nice one!!

L4Evah: Have you evah thought about having your very own home business!??

Me: I already run one

Me: you sell [her company's name] huh?

Me: that's cool, good for you

L4Evah: Awesome!! What biz do you have!?

Me: It's funny you ask

Me: I run a sales and leadership training company for network marketers

She didn't respond for an hour, but interestingly enough, wasn't open to hearing anything about what I do. I am 100% confident that a conversation with me would have earned her more money than if I would have bought the $20 product she was offering.

I understand that some would consider this to be a "customer first" interaction because she started with the product. However, "customer first" is different than being "product first."

Situation #2: All the Stuff Ever

My family and I went to Burbank to have dinner with my in-laws. There was a festival happening outside of the restaurant, so we wanted to walk around a bit and see what was going on. I passed by two booths run by different network marketers, in different companies. When I looked over to them, each space was covered in product. I started to walk over to one because the sign was cool, and then quickly walked away when I saw at least 50 different products. It was overwhelming.

I went to a booth across the street. It was a t-shirt company called, "Dude, Be Nice." There were three single t-shirts hung up with the front facing forward for all to see. There was one rack with six shirts, all the same size. There was a sign that said, "we have all sizes, just ask." I bought three shirts in five minutes.

Let's recap this experience: overwhelming with product is bad, and simple to buy is good.

> *Overwhelming with product is bad, and simple to buy is good.*

Situation #3: The Slam and Jam

I had just quit my corporate job and I thought it would be a good idea to reach out to a few people I knew who did network marketing. I connected with someone I used to work with.

I told her what I was thinking and that I had helped a few network marketers be successful. I told her my goal would be to help network marketers with their sales skills so they could be more successful. She responded with, "I don't think anyone needs that."

She then proceeded to tell me about how amazing her business was, and that I should join. I told her I was pretty sold on my own business idea. She backed off and then said, "well, would you like to try some of the products?" I got out of the conversation, although I'm not really sure how.

I told Charlie about this interaction. He responded, "It's like you walk into McDonald's and the cashier says, 'you need to buy this McDonald's store.' You say 'no,' and then they offer you a hamburger."

I laughed at his interpretation of this approach. I am ALL FOR inviting people to learn about the business and see if it's a good fit for them. However, I have a pro tip for you: if you are in a networking and relationship business, it's a really good idea NOT to slam the dreams of the person in front of you.

I am not a customer of any of these companies. I don't think any of these people did anything unethical, wrong, or offensive in any way. I love salespeople, remember? However, these interactions are not part of a thought process that considers the customer perspective.

This is why our philosophy is: customer first, team second, ego third.

The first consideration that we need to have is: "How does this help a customer have a better life?" The second consideration is: "How does this help my team be successful?" We never have to choose. If it's right for the customer, in most instances it's going to help your team be more successful.

Customer first, team second, ego third.

The last consideration is ego. You can still have ego in your business. We all do. As humans, we can't totally kick our ego to the curb. Our ego wants to be safe and comfortable. Our customers' and team members' interests must come before our ego.

I'll give you an example. My ego DOES NOT want to write this book. It wants to be safe and comfortable. It wants to protect me from a negative review, or someone saying, "Tasha Smith has no clue what she is talking about."

Instead of acting with those feelings in charge, I need to think about this question instead: "will this book be helpful for my customers?" I have clients who are eagerly awaiting an additional professional development tool for their team. I have corporate executives who are dying to be more customer centric, and they need a tool as well. And there are plenty of people out there who will be encouraged by this message.

So I'm going to do it! I bet you are glad, since you are in fact reading this book. Since I put my "customer first," what will happen to my team? More people will want to get 1-on-1 coaching to implement their systems and improve their skills. More people will want to join the hundreds who are already in our membership.

Remember my ego, who wanted to be comfortable and safe? Well, if you ask her some deeper questions, she also wants to have a significant impact in the world and massages every week. My ego, by stepping aside for a bit, actually gets everything she really wants.

Weeds Everywhere

Seven years ago, my husband Charlie and I bought our first home. We were excited. Our new home only had grass in the front yard, and there were some dirt planters with plants that didn't need attention.

We hired someone to come mow the lawn and that was it. Then two weeks later…the weeds came. They tried to overtake the planters! I called my mom. "What. Is. Happening?"

My mom calmly explained, "you have to pick the weeds to make your yard look nice." I responded, "That sounds like a lot of work."

Lucky for me, the gardener was happy to take on the weeds, and all was well. But I learned an important lesson.

To keep things nice, it TAKES WORK. It's worth it, though.

It's the same with customers. It is less work to send a few messages to see if they want to buy. It takes more work to invite them to an appointment.

It doesn't take much work at all to prescribe to the "some will, some won't, so what" philosophy where we can justify that they are simply not that interested. It takes more work to listen to them, and build value in a way that is personal to the potential customer.

If your home has weeds, it will be nearly impossible to sell. The worst part about an unkempt lawn is that it not only devalues your property, but also every property in the neighborhood.

The current market has the same tolerance for poor customer experience as the housing market does for weeds.

Weeds are much easier to pull when we do so proactively, when they are tiny. Once they take root and grow unchecked, it's much harder to fix the problem.

It's similar with customers. Yes, it's a little more work upfront to set your customers up for success. The trade-off is that you will then have more happy customers. Happy customers turn into superfans, who then turn into builders. It's easier to keep a happy customer than to find a new one. It's easier to enroll referrals than trying to make friends with strangers on the internet.

I am not advocating that you need to be perfect with customers. I am not perfect in this arena, so to do so would be completely hypocritical. For me, I know the improvement will be a lifelong process, as it is for any business. I still think as entrepreneurs we need to understand that our business is a never-ending pursuit to

Happy customers turn into superfans, who then turn into builders.

improve and to do things to the best of our current abilities. We will learn and improve over time. When we know better, we do better.

Commitments

"Customer First" network marketers and their teams experience more joy overall. Seeing customers rave about your products and company is extremely motivating. A bigger team with joy leads to bigger income levels, which gives you the freedom you really desire.

Freedom in any form—financial freedom, time freedom, etc.—is not an entitlement. Freedom is earned through hard work and commitment. Start with being fully committed to the following "customer first" philosophies.

Commitment #1: Commit to Skill Development

What do you get when you motivate an idiot? A motivated idiot. I didn't make up that joke—Jim Rohn did, so don't be mad at me! Yes, action is important. Enthusiasm is important. But to be "customer first" requires skill.

Having skill means that instead of vomiting product facts all over your potential customer, you are able to easily navigate that conversation in a way that makes you and them feel comfortable. Having skill means you can use your words, body language and eye contact to connect the dots and add value.

Commitment #2: Simplify the Way You Communicate

Our ego wants everything to be so complicated. When it's hard for others to understand, we feel smarter. Complications are not helpful to customers who are trying to solve their problems. If a fourth grader can't understand what you are saying, it's probably going to confuse your customers. Confused customers don't buy and get their problems solved.

Commitment #3: Encourage Action

It's the easy way out to give someone some information and then say, "let me know what you want to do." Some egos would argue that is kind, gracious, and actually is "customer first." That is a lie and a justification for low effort. Be confident and invite people to move forward. They are counting on you to believe in your product enough to say, "I think you would like it and won't regret it. Would you like me to help you place the order now so you get it by Friday?" Customers will follow your lead if you make a direct invitation to move forward. If they don't, at least everyone is on the same page and things don't get weird.

Commitment #4: Offer Without Attachment

Our job is to offer solutions, their job is to decide. Therefore, we NEVER prejudge or assume someone's priorities, budgets, or interest. One of my friends was a distributor for an essential oil company for a minute. This minute happened to be the same time I was invited to a class on how to use essential oils by a different friend. They actually worked with different companies. When I told my first friend who knew me well, she said, "wow, I never in a million years thought you would go for something like that." In the past four years, I have purchased over $8,000 worth of products. No, that is not a typo. Eight thousand dollars.

27

As Julia Roberts said in Pretty Woman, "You guys work on commission, right? Big mistake!" We all felt the pain when Julia's character was shunned from Beverly Hills stores. We knew deep down it wasn't right, but we do it every day without thinking, under the guise of "kindness" or "not being high pressure." In reality, that lack of inclusion and inviting is uncool and really lame. (Sorry friend, but I'd tell you to your face also.)

Prejudging is not kind. Assuming is not kind. Try this instead, "I don't want to make any assumptions so I ask everyone, is the complete kit a good fit for you and your family?" Don't forget to smile like you mean it. If they say, "no thanks, it's way too much stuff," then we can easily show other options.

Commitment #5: Processes

I don't know about you, but when I get tired, or even a bit discouraged, it's easy to cut corners. Create consistency for both you and your customers by outlining the steps that you do in a written process. Create processes for your team. It's not exactly fun, but it helps everyone help customers better. Chick-fil-A is known for having employees who provide value and an excellent customer experience. They have processes for everything so their employees don't need to spend so much time thinking, and can spend more time providing kindness and value to customers.

Commitment #6: Kick Fear to the Curb

Fear does not serve customers. Do not mistake passivity for caring about customers. The comment, "I don't want to bother them" might be a trigger that something is off and you need a

> *Fear does not serve customers.*

bit of skill, or it might be that you are avoiding a "no thank you" or a "no" answer. Neither will kill you. Improve your confidence by improving your skills. Then, be courageous. And you can only be brave if you are afraid first.

Commitment #7: Be Profitable

Be a smart business owner. Track your profits so you can feel successful. Spend your time on activities that lead to revenue in your business. When you buy a book like this or attend a training, implement! When you have a profitable business, you will be more confident and less desperate, inauthentic, or accidentally pushy. It's incredibly difficult to put customers first when finances aren't in order. Customers want to go to a clean, thriving restaurant more than one with a "going out of business" sign.

I understand that sometimes legs fall apart, and that there are waves in your business. I have seen them in my own businesses over my life and it can be really hard. We can't completely avoid tough times in our business. Still, be committed to thinking and acting like a profitable business owner, and your customers will feel it.

Customer First Takeaways

- To be "customer first" is to look at our business through the eyes of the customer.

- Being "customer first" is not a passive process that happens simply because we are nice people.

- Being "customer first" comes from a commitment to be brave, take extra time to think, and improve skills.

CHAPTER 3

"CUSTOMER FIRST" CREATES TEAMS

All this talk about customers, and you are still saying, "but Tasha, this is a recruiting business. I can't reach the highest levels unless I am a great recruiter and leader."

We don't need to start with why network marketing is amazing. You and I both are on "Team Network Marketing" already. And we aren't quite ready to discuss how to explain "the opportunity." We need to first remember that our potential builders are humans, and we need to look at the world through their perspective without being defensive.

We need to take a look at why people launch their network marketing business AND why people don't want to "do network marketing."

Let's do a quick brainstorm as to why people resist joining network marketing as a business builder.

1. They don't want to be salesy or pushy

2. They don't know if the product is good enough

3. They think it might be a scam. This usually comes from overpromoting how successful someone will be with very little work

4. They don't have time

5. They prefer to be told what to do and to have predictability in their career

6. The timing isn't right for them to start the business

Do you see how many of these stem from poor network marketing customer experiences?

So many people in network marketing say "it's a numbers game." It's true-ish, but also incomplete. You need to know the math so you don't get personally attached to people not being interested, but ultimately, it's a "people game."

I'm going to rant for a minute: never use words that dishonor your customers. When you say, "It's a numbers game" be careful. Would you want your customers to hear you say that?

Remember that for new builders, their first customers are their own mother, sister, neighbor, and best friend.

The sales process MUST be executed in such a way that they do not feel "salesy" or "pushy" because they are working with their social circle. Some network marketing circles will shame you and tell you it doesn't matter what your social circle thinks.

I don't know about you, but what my best friends think of me DOES matter. They don't get to make decisions for me, and if they didn't fully understand my rationale, it would not deter me. However, as humans we are drawn to tribes, so despite all of my "enlightenment" I honestly do care about what my parents, family, and close friends think of me. I want them to be proud of me, not think I'm some kind of sales weirdo.

Many people who resist network marketing do so because there is a particular negative experience that left a bad taste in their mouths. Even though I am not an active network marketer, my first experience was so incredibly positive it has colored and shaped my view of the industry. I believe network marketers are awesome, because I am always around awesome network marketers. What if my first conscious experience was with L4Evah, and that's what I believed network marketing to be?

Many people have a story of some relative or high school friend who approached them while "doing the numbers game." The copy and paste approach turned them off and they don't want to spend their days around awkward and embarrassing behavior. Do you see how the major objection doesn't have as much to do with "network marketing" as it has to do with the customer experience?

Recently, I did a survey of some clients to see how they started, and it might surprise you to hear the results. This group consists of committed network marketers who have invested in their skill development, so they are definitely the people you want on your team. I got 50 responses pretty quickly. 8% started as a customer and builder at the same time. 16% started as a business builder. The rest, 76% of committed network marketers, started as a CUSTOMER first.

A "customer first" sales process will make building a team so much easier because a high percentage of your future team will come from your customers, not from people who come right out of the gate to start a business.

A high percentage of your future team will come from your customers.

The Recruiting Assembly Line

You want to recruit builders. 46% of Americans don't have an extra $500 to their name. Many people are open to a side hustle to improve their family's life.

It should be a no brainer, but unfortunately, it's not. There are a bunch of factors outside of your control, like their schedule, their interests, their personality, and other factors as well. But there is one factor that is within your control: the recruiting assembly line.

Let's back up though and remember how assembly lines work. If you do step 4 before step 1, your end result is wonky. Yes, wonky is a technical term.

I know that we would all like to think that people make decisions logically. In fact, since WE are so logical, we assume everyone is so logical. *insert eye roll here*

Spoiler alert: We aren't logical. Research shows time and time again that decisions are made emotionally, and then justified logically.

For example, you are walking through Target on an escape from the kids. We know we can get milk at the grocery store, but I agree, you should get it at Target. There is a t-shirt that says, "I'm done adulting today" and this shirt "gets you." It makes you feel more connected and a little justified, so you want the shirt. You know if you buy the shirt, you will feel better and maybe even happy. Now that you have all the feels, you justify it with logic like, "it's such a good deal." You didn't exactly buy it because it was a good deal. If that were true, we would just buy everything that is on sale.

Humans make decisions emotionally in most cases, and justify them logically. How then does this apply to business builders deciding to join your team?

Potential builders need to have certain **feelings** before they get to work. And these feelings work in an assembly line format.

1. **I trust this person**

2. **This is a freaking awesome product**

3. **I know people who will love this too**

4. **I can do this (and enjoy it)**

5. **I can make money**

According to Gallup's extensive research on what people want from a leader, they want *trust, compassion, stability and hope.* You can establish those feelings for customers AND builders (if you follow what's in the next sections), thereby building a bigger base of potential builders. This is because even your CUSTOMERS see you as a leader they can follow.

I trust this person.

If people feel like you care about them when you approach them, they will trust you more. We need to demonstrate this not only in the recruiting process, but also the sales process, because this is where they are likely to connect with you the first time.

This is a freaking awesome product.

This is a good business BECAUSE it's a good product. Nobody wants to represent a crappy product. They want to feel good about the results their customers are getting. They want to feel hopeful that this is going to solve problems. They want to be proud of what they represent.

This often happens in the sales process. If you happen to have someone who you approach, or who approaches you regarding the business first, don't skip steps. Take a few extra minutes to build product conviction.

I know people who will love this too.

As you are explaining how your products solve problems and helps meet goals, a peculiar thing is happening inside the mind of your potential builder. They are naturally thinking of people who will also benefit.

In your conversation, you will ask them about their goals and explain products. They are applying this knowledge to themselves AND their loved ones. Customers will continue to order when their FAMILY needs the products more than if the customer themselves needs the product.

Let's say you are talking about a shake that they can drink when they don't have time to eat a healthy meal. It's not a far stretch for me to think of my brother who doesn't like to eat breakfast, my husband who only has a 30-minute lunch break and likes to take walks instead of sitting in the lunchroom, and my mom.

This is a seed planted toward growing the business or referrals, and it happens under the surface. As you know from an earlier chapter, I know very little about gardening. But I do know this much: the seed is under the surface. The seed starts to grow without anyone seeing it, so we need to keep watering until it rises above the surface.

I can do this.

You have no doubt heard the word "duplication" over and over again if you have been in the industry for more than five minutes. Duplication is simply the fact that other people can also use your process to get results.

Potential builders need to experience the sales process and feel, "Ok, this seems simple enough and now I am wanting to buy this product. I think I could do this too."

Remember, they have already been thinking about people in the last step of the assembly line.

It really helps if your steps are written out in a checklist or an outline of some sort so everything is simple and organized in one place.

I can make money at this.

Potential builders need to believe that people will buy this stuff, that they can do it, and that they will be compensated fairly.

Your confidence, belief and enthusiasm will be contagious. You don't need to overstate the opportunity. The compensation needs to be fair and they need to know what they need to do to get paid.

You might be wondering why this is the last step in the assembly line. It's because it means nothing if they don't believe the first four steps.

Your confidence, belief and enthusiasm will be contagious.

Many times people will come "for the income opportunity." You, as the leader, get super excited and explain the compensation plan. They go as quickly as they came. What happened!?! The assembly line is out of order.

Remember that they are likely to start with people they know. We need to go through the right order so they don't get a mind bend over "making money off the people I know."

They will be more positive about their experience if they see compensation as "getting to help my family and friends and by the way I also get paid well, that's awesome!"

Customer First Takeaways

• Many people resist network marketing as a business builder because the sales process is sloppy and they can't see themselves doing it.

• From leaders, people want trust, compassion, stability and hope, and you can build this in a "customer first" sales process.

• Three quarters of your future team is incubating in your customer base.

• Building product conviction will improve the likelihood that your builder starts and sticks around through the learning curve of the business.

• Following a simple sales process that makes the customer feel amazing increases their confidence and hope to earn money while doing something fun.

CHAPTER 4

IMPACT BEFORE INCOME

I have a love-hate relationship with numbers in my business. I love them when they are good, and I hate them when they are bad!

When I started my coaching practice, I was creating something out of nothing. I have always been competitive and goal-oriented. I kept looking at my revenue and it wasn't growing. I started getting discouraged, frustrated, and stressed out. Can you relate with this?

A watched pot doesn't boil. And a watched back office doesn't grow. Watching my numbers wasn't going to make my numbers grow. Finding customers with problems and solving them is the only way to move the numbers, but I didn't understand this at the time.

So there I was, feeling discouraged, frustrated, and stressed out. How do you think I presented myself to potential clients? Discouraged, frustrated, and stressed out. How do you think they responded to me? They backed away slowly.

With potential clients backing away from me, what do you think happened to my revenue and my business? Nothing. Literally nothing.

Then my brilliant business coach, Heather, saved me from myself. She spends most Tuesdays saving me from myself. She taught me the most powerful concept I have learned in leadership: impact comes before income.

I had known for a long time that I needed to measure my "performance indicators." This is just a fancy way of saying, "know the most important numbers in your business."

It's just like when you go to the doctor and he measures your blood pressure, temperature, and weight. In the medical field, these are called your vitals. In athletics, it's your statistics. I played basketball in college and they measured our playing time, assists, points, rebounds and turnovers.

Impact comes before income.

To improve our business, we need to also look at our statistics so we can improve them, just like an athlete would.

Heather explained to me that there are leading indicators and lagging indicators. Huh? I learned a lot in my MBA, but not this. Or maybe I was distracted passing notes to my friends…

What is a lagging indicator?

It's the result. It's the thing that comes last. New customers, client renewals, revenue, and income were my "lagging indicators of success." Yours are your rank, income, and overall team volume.

What is a leading indicator?

For me, leading indicators include things like new connections, appointments, quick wins for potential clients, clarity or results for current clients, and overall positive feedback. The leading indicator is the thing that creates or causes the lagging indicator. In your business, you'll have similar leading indicators of success, like how many new connections you have added or how many people you have attending events. If you don't have connections or people at appointments, you don't have anyone to sell to.

Why does this matter?

If all we track is results, that's better than tracking nothing. However, when results happen, it's already too late for you to make a change. I would need to go into a time machine at least 60-90 days back to increase the activities that would create today's sales.

All business boils down to this essence: find a problem, solve it, and then get paid. Our income is a direct reflection of how many problems our efforts have solved.

When I focused on my sales, I would feel like every interaction had a ton of pressure on it. I didn't listen as well, I had way more of an agenda, and I couldn't help but apply pressure to the person I was speaking to.

Instead, Heather redirected me to focus on IMPACT. The definition of impact that we are using here is not like a plane crashing. It's something that has a significant or major effect.

What if every day, our goal was to positively impact people with our business? I love to encourage people. I have said since I was 22 years old that my mission was to sell hope. This "impact before income" philosophy resonated with me. I still had revenue goals. I still had profit goals. I still measured my statistics in my business on a weekly and monthly basis. But I stopped looking at them every day. Instead, I set out to impact five people per day. My revenue tripled the next month. Then it doubled again. I couldn't believe it.

The best part was that it felt so amazing because I knew I was actually helping people. Impacting more people, feeling happier, and making more money...how on earth could this work so well?

How to Stay Motivated

"People say that motivation doesn't last. Neither does bathing. That's why we recommend it daily."

—Zig Ziglar

As entrepreneurs, we don't have a boss paying us a salary and giving us ultimatums. For most of us, this is very different from how we grew up. Our parents told us what to do and when to do it. Our teachers did the same. Our coaches made our entire team run if we were one minute late for practice. Then at work, we were given a schedule, a set of tasks or goals, and we needed to reach them...or else. We are used to external motivation.

It really didn't matter if we were motivated, we HAD to show up. So as motivation went up and down in our lives, our obligation to show up weathered the lack of motivational storms as we continued to build success. We simply showed up and did the job.

But now, we are entrepreneurs, and the job of motivating us falls on... *gulp*...us. The good news is that our focus on customers first will drastically improve our motivation.

To understand motivation, we must first understand burnout. Burnout comes from feeling like all of your hard work doesn't matter. It's that feeling that no matter how hard you work, nothing will change. For example, teachers get burnt out because they might work so hard with a kid, only to have their hard work be undone by a terrible home situation. It's been said that so many people quit right before the breakthrough. Why does that happen? I think it's burnout. It's because people feel like they are working very hard for no effect so they throw in the towel.

> *Our focus on customers first will drastically improve our motivation.*

We need to fight off burnout while increasing our motivation, so we show up consistently, and get great results in our business. No problem, right?

In *Drive: The Surprising Truth About What Motivates Us,* Daniel Pink shares his findings on how to stay motivated, and how to motivate others in their work. For the purposes of this book, we will focus on keeping ourselves motivated, and revisit this a bit when we talk about recruiting and leadership.

Once our basic needs are met, we are driven by autonomy, mastery, and purpose. The good news is that network marketing draws out our inner motivation by design. We simply need to keep our focus on the things that excite us.

Autonomy

Autonomy is our desire to be self-directed. We want to be masters of our own destiny. We come out of the womb this way. We are always striving for independence. We want to do things the way we want to do them. This always reminds me of when my daughter Zoey was two, and we would try to get her out of her carseat. She would slap our hands and scream, "Zoey! By! Self!" Even though everything our kids want to do themselves take so much longer than if we did it for them, they seem to insist. Well…until they know how to do it. Then it's our turn again.

The network marketing industry encourages autonomy because entrepreneurs get to set their own schedule and "be their own boss." Sure, there are some downsides if people don't have experience regulating themselves professionally, but this makes network marketing highly motivating.

Yes, I'm sure you have an upline and a corporate structure that provides some guidance. But remember, once you have the basics down you are free to serve customers in the best ways you think are possible. Have fun and enjoy testing different ideas, ones you learn from others or create yourself.

Mastery

Mastery is our desire to get better skills. Why are we so motivated to learn musical instruments or play sports even though we won't be paid for it? These activities are motivating because we get the opportunity to improve our skills. We also gravitate toward things we can do, and see ourselves improve at.

Let's say you and your friends are going out dancing in Los Angeles on a Friday night. I would politely decline, explaining that I need to take care of my kids and I'm a responsible business owner. However, let's say you are on an ice hockey team and you need a sub for the day. And the league is in Los Angeles. I would respond, "Great! Where do I pay?"

What's the difference in my motivation? I can't clap to a song in church, let alone dance to a rhythm. Dancing will likely lead to me looking foolish. When I play hockey, I can play successfully and I get better and better as I play more consistently. Therefore, I am more motivated to play hockey. The "I don't have time to do that" objection disappears.

Network marketing requires a basic set of skills most people can do, and as income grows, a new set of skills emerge. According to one of my clients, Daniela, it's like a video game. As soon as you master one level, the game pops you up to the next level, which requires a new set of tools and a new strategy built upon what you have already learned.

Keep yourself motivated by mastering one skill at a time. If you need a list of skills to master, I have you covered. There are two sets of skills: one is customer-facing, and one is team-facing.

Customer-facing skills: basic time management and goal setting, setting appointments, closing sales, customer retention, lead generation, recruiting and launching new builders.

Team-facing skills: Time management and goal setting as a leader, gaining agreement, coaching on skill development, coaching on goal setting and achieving, team culture, and developing leaders.

At first glance, this could appear overwhelming. But this is actually good news! Once you know the skills to master, you will be much more likely to seek development in that area.

Purpose

Purpose refers to our desire to be significant, or to be a part of something bigger than ourselves. My sweet husband, Charlie, has always professed that he hates baseball. A few years ago, he left the home in a frenzy to find a Dodgers hat. What motivated him to spend money on a team who plays a sport that he "hates?" The Dodgers were in the World Series, and he wanted to be a part of something bigger. All of a sudden I heard phrases like, "we got a home run." Unfortunately, the Dodgers lost in the World Series, but the phenomenon was not lost upon me.

People who have network marketing businesses have an easy time aligning with the fact that their products help people. They get to be their own boss, but they are also part of a movement that is much bigger than themselves. Many network marketing companies have strong philanthropic commitments, further aligning builders with purpose and significance.

Keep yourself motivated by focusing on how your products or the income-earning part of your business makes people's lives better. Stay motivated by plugging into the mission of your company and attending company and team events.

The Impact Journal

It's been said that we have a tendency to remember what we should forget, and forget what we should remember. I think this is really true in our businesses. We are constantly looking at the next thing we need to improve, or perhaps at mistakes from the past.

The problem with this mental strategy is that whatever we focus on grows. If we focus on mistakes, mistakes grow. If we constantly tell ourselves we need to strive for more, this feeling of inadequacy grows.

This is why Heather prescribed to me "the impact journal."

What is it?

The impact journal can be a simple journal you get at the Dollar Store, a beautiful leather journal, a notebook, the top of your planner, or an app on your phone.

Each day, write down the people in your life who you positively impacted through your business.

Did you encourage a team member? Write that down.

43

Did you make a sale? Write that down.

Is someone excited about a new product that was released and is going to order it? Write that down.

Did you get a great testimonial from a customer? Write that down.

Was someone's problem solved or goal met that day? Just write it down.

Each day, write down the people in your life who you positively impacted through your business.

Why is it important?

The impact journal keeps us motivated. It's not an assignment that you need to turn in for your boss or upline. Since it's self-directed, it triggers our need for autonomy.

Over time, your impacts change. When I started coaching, my impacts were, "Katherine had a great class." Today, my impact might be that someone had 100+ people on a team meeting that we made a plan to promote. By writing down your impacts, you will see your mastery grow and change. I hate to break it to you, but you will likely always have that twinge of not being as good as you "should be." That's simply because there is truly no ceiling in entrepreneurship. The impact journal reminds you that you are doing a great job.

Also, the impact journal reinforces your purpose. We all want to feel significant and that we make a difference in people's lives. You will be keeping a private, running log of all of the people (customers and builders) that you are helping. The evidence is there on paper: you are making a difference. There will be times where your revenue is lower than you would like it to be and it can cause you to be emotional. The impact journal grounds us and ensures that we feel successful so we stay in action and keep our momentum going, no matter what is happening around us.

Last, the impact journal will keep you focused on the leading indicators of success. This will keep you focused on CREATING instead of getting distracted by results that you can't change.

Friend, as you go through this book, I want to encourage you to focus on your daily impact in your community—both local and online. If you are working part-time, focus on three impacts per day. If you are working full-time, focus on five impacts per day. If you find yourself with a lack of focus, check your impact journal. I bet you have forgotten to take it out recently.

Just three impacts a day for a whole year is over 1,000 positive impacts in a year. What do you think your business would be like if you had 1,000 impacts per year? Distraction is the enemy of your business. Shame is part of the same villain crew. Shame is that whisper that says, "you aren't doing enough." Kick shame and distraction to the curb by keeping your impact journal.

The impact journal works every single time to jumpstart motivation, create results in your business and increase joy. Every, single, time.

Kick shame and distraction to the curb by keeping your impact journal.

When you write in your impact journal, you will see more happiness, more focus, more results and more income in your business. Another added perk is that when you focus on impact and THEN income, you will never come across as "that salesperson."

Customer First Takeaways

- Your income is a direct reflection of the impact your business has on the world.

- To increase your income, focus on increasing your impact.

- We are motivated by autonomy, which is our quest for independence.

- We are motivated by mastery, which is our quest to be better.

- We are motivated by purpose, which is our quest to be significant and a part of something bigger.

- Write down three impacts per day in a journal to stay motivated, increase your income, and never come across as "salesy".

SECTION 2

CUSTOMER FIRST SALES

CHAPTER 5

THE BEGINNING AND THE END MATTER

I will never forget the last 10 seconds of the Southern California Girls Basketball Playoffs in 1997. In my senior year of high school, our basketball team was one of the favorites in our division to win the Southern California title. The other favorite was our rival, Valley Christian. Before meeting Valley in the semi-finals, our record was 20-5—with two of those losses being to Valley. They would be our toughest opponent in the play-offs.

The end of the game ended in dramatic fashion. One of our forwards got the rebound of a missed free throw and quickly passed to Ann-Marie, who was playing point guard at the time. I was sprinting up the left side of the court, calling for the ball. Ann-Marie passed it. I took two dribbles with my left hand, squared up, and hit the 3-pointer at the buzzer!

Ann-Marie sprinted over and gave me the biggest hug of our lives. I will never forget it. I still can't believe I made that shot.

There was one problem. Actually, there were 22 problems. We were down by more than 20 points at the time I made that 3-point shot.

There is an old adage, "it's not how you start, it's how you finish."

I learned that day that the start, the middle, AND the end matter.

I "closed" that game, like a boss. But my flawless technique and eye of the tiger didn't matter. We had not built a foundation to put us in a position to win at the end.

Sales is like this as well. A favorable outcome for your customer to solve their problems and for your business to grow does not only happen at the end. It starts at the beginning.

This is why it's true that we need to "always be closing." But remember in the last section we talked about closing to be more about uniting than about forcing our way. We need to "always be uniting."

The beginning of our sales process is the FIRST time we introduce the idea of our products to the potential customer. We must start making the buying process enjoyable from this point onward.

What do I mean "enjoyable?" Can sales be enjoyable?!?! Of course it can! People enjoy buying things that they like and find useful. Business owners love to see their customers' glee and delight, and they also love to be successful in finding solutions for people's problems.

Customers HATE working with inauthentic, pushy salespeople, but they LOVE working with someone who cares about them and operates as a trusted advisor.

There are five keys to making sales an enjoyable process for you and the customer, and they will be outlined in the next five chapters. The five keys can and should be applied in more situations than just enrolling a new customer. There are many "sales" you make as a leader.

A "sales conversation" is when you are discussing products with a potential customer. This is obvious.

A "recruiting conversation" is a conversation where the product is an idea that starting a network marketing business will be fun and impactful. The five keys apply to this conversation as well.

A "coaching conversation" is a conversation with a team member to mentor them and guide them in their business. Here, you are "selling" action. Using the five keys as an outline for your coaching process will increase the likelihood that your team member moves into action instead of you becoming a network marketing therapist.

For the purposes of this book, we will use customer examples but you can make adjustments for anything. Want to have a conversation with your spouse about why your family needs to take a nice vacation next year? Use the five keys.

The five keys are:

1. Set up an appointment (don't sell on the fly)

2. Give an agenda

3. Gain input

4. Personalize features and benefits

5. Make it easy to buy

Just like all four quarters of a basketball game matter, following each of these five keys will drastically improve your confidence, improve the fun factor of your business, and decrease stress for you and the customer.

You may run into some situations where you aren't able to do all five of the keys because the potential customer isn't responding. That's ok. If plan A doesn't work, don't worry because the alphabet has 26 letters.

You can combine any tools that you think are helpful WITH the five keys. For example, if you love to give people samples, give them a sample AND use the five keys. If the "tool" your company uses is a "presentation" simply adjust your wording and flow to use the slides in conjunction with the five keys. Do you like to do group events that are typically called parties, classes, or socials? Great! Use the five keys to improve the effectiveness of the event. Are you doing a three-way call for your team member? Use the five keys.

Imagine that you feel confident on how to structure every major conversation in your business. Imagine making sales on at least half of your first appointments with potential customers. Imagine how you would feel if you could triple the amount of customers you personally enrolled and retained because your conversations were effective. And now, imagine if your downline could do the same.

Are you ready?

Great. Let's freaking do this.

CHAPTER 6

DON'T SELL ON THE FLY

Imagine for a moment, you are at the park with your family. You are wearing your company hat, your company shirt, and your keys are on your company keychain. You strike up a conversation with someone. And what luck! Guess what comes up in conversation? Your company! (Imagine that...)

The person you are speaking with asks about what you do, and what is your response? Be honest!

If you are like most people, you are laughing a little right now imagining this scenario. When I ask this question, most people respond with, "I vomit all over them." Maybe this is you, or maybe it's someone on your team.

Most people get so excited that someone is "interested" in their product or company that this excitement and enthusiasm takes over. The network marketer starts spewing features and benefits into the space between them and the innocent person standing in front of them.

It reminds me of the time in the middle of the night when my daughter Zoey was a year old and she was crying, which wasn't like her. I held her and to my surprise, Zoey puked on me. There was so much that it went down my shirt and somehow made it down my pants. YUCK!

After being puked on, what do you think my reaction was? Blank face, and slowly walk away backwards.

The same thing happens to your customer when you vomit on them about your company. When we see their blank face, how do we typically respond?

Oh, we talk faster! Or we completely clam up, knowing what we have just done.

If you are the first person, you are feeling your internal alarm going off. "Oh no! I'm losing them! Talk FASTER!" Now we are talking about all of the humanitarian work our company does, perhaps we are showing our friend's before and after pictures, or shoving samples in their face.

And more often than not, they start backing away faster.

Or maybe you are the second type of person, and your instinct is to stop talking. You went from very excited to very awkward, very quickly. You know you have gone too far, and so you retreat.

Either way, it's awkward. And does this person end up buying?

Earlier, we agreed that your product has life-changing properties. When your customer walks away overwhelmed and without your life changing products, who has missed out the most?

Sure, you might have "lost" a sale. But THEY are the ones without the life-changing product. Unfortunately, despite all of your enthusiasm, they are not likely to solve their problems. The competition for your products is not other products. Your real competition is clients who take NO action at all. Doing nothing is easier for them than investing in something life-changing.

They have their money, but they also still have their problems.

Try This Instead...

Instead of immediately pitching the products, let's set up an appointment. The customer isn't in the space to make a decision and you aren't likely in the space to be organized.

Put yourself in the role of the customer for a few minutes. Imagine for a moment your business or career is going so well that you need to hire a virtual assistant to take all of the administrative work off your plate.

This is a dream, until it starts to feel like a nightmare. Do you even know how to write a contract for someone like that?

You decide to suspend your panic while you go to attend your cousin's wedding. You end up at a table with a contracts lawyer. What luck!

Does this lawyer tell you everything that you need to know about contracts at the dinner table? Of course not? Why not? Because you would be overwhelmed and it's not the time or the place to go over this information.

Who misses out? If you said the lawyer, I'm sorry, friend, but you are wrong. You are the one who misses out. You are the one who needs to understand how contracts work, and you are the one who doesn't have the expertise.

It's a good thing our lawyer friend doesn't vomit contract law on you at the wedding. Instead, she sets up an appointment. And who benefits? You do. She does. Your future virtual assistant also wins. Everyone wins.

What if we did the same thing? What if instead of spewing all of the facts and enthusiasm about our products or services we just set up an appointment?

How would that make a customer feel?

How would that make you feel?

And if your customer feels amazing, and you feel amazing, how would that make your monthly check feel?

Wait, do monthly checks even have feelings?

What to Say to Set Up an Appointment

Instead of vomiting or not saying anything at all, we can respond with something like this:

> **"Usually what I do is set up a time to go over your goals, a little about the company, and the most popular kits. My part will take about 30 minutes. You don't**

have to get anything, but if you see something you like, of course I'll help you order it. Is that something you would be open to?"

How do you think your customer would respond?

If you are nodding your head, you are not alone, my friend.

Why do you think they would respond this way? Let's look at each part of this appointment invitation from the customer's perspective.

"Usually what I do…"

This phrase establishes that appointments are normal. This conversation that you are having with them is not out of the norm and you are playing it cool. Don't forget, when someone is interested in your product, BE COOL.

By saying "usually what I do," "typically what I do," or any variation of this phrase, you are helping the customer feel more comfortable.

Some people like to be unique, but most people use "social proof" as a test for whether or not people are going to move forward.

People feel so much more comfortable knowing that others have gone where they are about to go, and they didn't die.

By using the phrase, "usually what I do" you are creating a comfortable, relaxed atmosphere for the potential customer.

"…set up a time to go over your _____ goals, a little about the company, and the most popular kits."

In this part, we are going to tell the customer exactly what we are going to do in the conversation. Many network marketers will say, "I try to set up appointments but they don't want to do it." More often than not, the invitation is something like this, "would you like to set up an appointment?"

Customers aren't naturally going to want to come to an appointment where they don't know what's happening, or how long it is going to take.

With this agenda, we are going to tell the customer the conversation is going to start with THEIR goals. Remember, customer FIRST.

There are a few variations on the "goal part" of the agenda because it's going to depend on your product line. If you are in the health and wellness industry, I recommend, "set up a time to go over your health goals." If you are in an industry that isn't goal oriented, I recommend something like, "set up a time to talk about what's important to you when it comes to choosing make-up." The first part of the agenda is going to be 100% about the customer, which is perfect. It's his or her favorite topic of conversation.

"My part will take about 30 minutes."

By giving them a timeline, we are building more trust. People are busy and are likely to say they are "too busy" if they don't know how long it's going to take.

If your part takes more than 30 minutes, you will need to tell them the truth. You may need to say, "my part will take about 45 minutes" or even longer. Whatever the time frame, tell your customer the truth. This will help you when you do the actual appointment, and continue the comfortable atmosphere when you meet.

> *By giving them a timeline, we are building more trust.*

"You don't have to get anything, but if you see something you like, of course I'll help you order it."

This part of the agenda is to remove pressure. Customers need to know that you aren't going to hold a gun to their head to buy, but if they want to buy, they can!

This way, you are not "selling" anything. You are simply offering them an opportunity to do something they already want to do: shop.

"Is that something you would be open to?"

Before we move on to the actual setting of the appointment, we want to do something very few network marketers do: ask for consent.

I had a client once who got added without permission to 273 groups for the same company! That was over two years ago so I can't even imagine how many groups have added her today!!!

How do you think she feels about this particular company? Not great. But it's not even inviting that is the issue. It's the inviting without consent that is so frustrating. And I know you don't like doing this either.

So we are going to be different. We are going to ask for consent. Use questions like:

- Is that something you would be open to?
- Would that be helpful?
- How does that sound?

If possible, stay away from, "is that something you are interested in?" Very few people are interested in an appointment like this. However, many people see themselves as "open."

Pro Tip: Give a Choice of Two Times

Once someone says, "yes" to your consent question, give them a choice of two times. Keep it simple. If you ask, "when is good for you?" your customer is likely going to want to get back to you.

Look at your schedule and say something like, "I can do tomorrow at 4pm or Friday at 10am. Which would work better for you?"

If neither work, offer two more until they find one that works. We will cover the "choice of two" in way more detail in a later chapter. But for now, what you need to know is that this makes it so much easier on their brain.

Could you see yourself using this approach to schedule two appointments per week? Using the "secrets" you will learn in the next four chapters, we have found that many people make sales on over 60% of their first appointments!

2 appointments X 4 weeks = 8 appointments

8 appointments X 60% sales rate = 5 new customers per month

This is completely manageable for someone working part-time. I know some of you reading this book are working full-time and are thinking, "it's on." I agree, this is exciting.

Customer First Takeaways

- "Selling on the fly" does not help customers solve their problems.

- Be cool—offer an appointment instead.

- When offering an appointment, give them an agenda, tell them how long it's going to take, remove pressure, gain their agreement, and give a choice of two times.

CHAPTER 7

NO SURPRISES

I am a network marketer's dream customer. I love buying things that are high quality, especially if I like the salesperson.

But I am NOT adaptable. I remember when I took the Gallup's Strengthsfinder Assessment. I unlocked all 34 talents. Guess what was 34-of-34? Adaptability.

I called my mom. "Hey Mom! Want to hear something funny? I took a test and #34 out of 34 talents is adaptability."

She responded, "I could have told you that, you didn't need to pay for a test." As Homer Simpson says, "DOH!"

I really like to know the plan. I like to know where we are going, and what our goal is when we get there. It makes me feel comfortable and I have something to be excited about.

And so how does this "dream customer" sit down with a network marketer with a great product, and it ends without a sale?

I will tell you how this happens: I get super freaked out when there are surprises I haven't prepared for.

I wonder if this story sounds familiar to you, from either perspective.

I was new in my coaching business. I was hustling, getting referrals and setting up as many complimentary coaching calls as I could. I wanted to get out of the house, so I looked up networking groups that were close to my home. I found one pretty quickly and the best part is that they were meeting for lunch at a rib place. Double win!

I was so awkward. It was a situation I had never been in before so I didn't really know how to act or what to do. I met this guy, let's call him Bob. I don't remember his name.

Bob seemed like one of the leaders of the group and he was very nice. The networking event was pretty simple. We listened to a speaker. We gave each other referrals. I thought giving people I didn't know referrals was super weird since I didn't really know that much about what people did.

Bob was very interested in me and very kind. He told me he works in "customer relations management" or something like that. Cool Bob, good job.

He asked me if I wanted to go for coffee to brainstorm marketing techniques. I didn't, really. I asked him if this was a sales appointment of some sort. He assured me it wasn't. I was new so after some persistence on his part, I agreed.

We met at the Starbucks closest to my home. He asked me a few questions about what I did and I still didn't know what was going on. I felt very much like he was in control. He bought the coffee which made me feel even more uncomfortable.

Then Bob launched into his "presentation." He proceeded to tell me about his amazing product that aided with customer retention. Then he talked about how if I just got three people who got three people…he used playing cards as if recruiting was a game. It was weird.

Bob wanted to know if I wanted to move forward. Nope, customer gifts are not something that I had as a priority at this time.

"Well Tasha, if customer gifts are not something in your budget, let me tell you how you can get your gifts for free by getting three people who get three people…"

Umm…

I was a "no sale." The bummer part is that I actually really liked (and still like) the product line and I think it's very smart.

Then why was I a lost sale?

I didn't trust Bob.

Looking back, I felt like Bob pulled a "switcheroo" on me. He didn't give me full disclosure on the appointment. He made it sound like he was a consultant of some sorts, who just wanted to brainstorm with a fellow entrepreneur.

Maybe I should give Bob a little grace, he did follow Key #1 of this section.

However, I would have been so much more comfortable if when I arrived, he had just shared with me what I could expect during our conversation.

Give an Agenda

To positively impact more customers, we need to establish trust, compassion, stability and hope.

At the beginning of each appointment, for the love of God, please give your customers an agenda.

Don't be like Bob. If your name is Bob and you are reading this, I'm sorry for using your name. You can be like yourself. Just don't be like that other guy.

To positively impact more customers, we need to establish trust, compassion, stability and hope.

Let's rewrite my story about Bob. I still go to the networking event and don't really feel comfortable in this new space. He invites me to coffee to talk about marketing ideas. He is still grateful for the meeting and offers to pay for the coffee. I still reluctantly agree.

This time, he starts with an agenda.

"Tasha, the reason I invited you here today is that I help small businesses retain their customers with some marketing ideas. I would love to hear your goals for your business, and the ideas you already have for keeping in touch and top of mind with previous customers so they stay loyal.

After that, if you are open, I'd like to share with you the solutions that I have. If you think they are a good fit for you, great. I can give you direction on how to move forward. If it's not a good fit, that works too. Mostly, I want to stay as connected as possible to as many small business owners as possible. How does that sound?"

I might have left. Or I might have stayed and ordered. And while my order would have been tiny then, I would probably be using his largest plan now and referring out his business like crazy.

So what does this look like in your network marketing business? At the beginning of a 1-on-1 or group event, just lay out the details of the agenda to make the person/people you are speaking to much more comfortable.

> *"Just to review, today we are going to go over your _____ goals, a little about the company, and the most popular kits. My part will take about 30 minutes. You don't have to get anything, but if you see something you like, I'll help you order it today. How does that sound?"*

How do you think this makes a customer feel?

What you will notice when you start sharing the agenda at the beginning of each appointment, is that your customer's shoulders will relax and their facial expressions will lighten up. Their eye contact will increase. And they will nod their head.

Let's break down the components of this agenda, and why it works so well.

> *"Just to review, today we are going to go over your _____ goals, a little about the company, and the most popular kits. My part will take about 30 minutes."*

Ideally, these are the same bullet points that you said when you set up the appointment. This gives your customer the feeling of stability. They know that you will be the same from interaction to interaction. They now are putting you in a different category of people than other salespeople they have ever met with. You are trustworthy, reliable, and respectful.

61

You follow through on commitments. This is an essential quality of a good human.

"You don't have to get anything, but if you see something you like, I'll help you order it today. How does that sound?"

The best time to address the elephant in the room is the beginning. A lot of network marketers struggle with educating the customer and then feeling bad by asking them to buy at the end. This problem is now eliminated.

When you remove the pressure to buy, WHILE encouraging them to note things they like, you are shifting this from a "sales atmosphere" to a "buying atmosphere." Customers hate to be sold, but they LOVE to buy.

Your potential customer will almost always nod their head up and down, indicating that they agree.

You might have noticed that I added the word "today" to the original appointment setting outline. This was on purpose. It's not helpful to you or the customer to follow up forever. Today is the highest point of their motivation. Ordering today will lead to the fastest results for your customer. So we set the agreement that if they see something they like, they will order it today because it just makes sense.

In the first 60 seconds of your 1-on-1 or group event, your customers have JUST agreed that if they see something they like, they will order today. Eureka! No pressure, no "creating urgency" ploys. It's just a simple agreement and everyone is on the same page because the agreement is fair.

This sentence seems simple enough, but as your guide, I would be remiss if I didn't show you where most people make mistakes.

Trap #1: Changing to "there is no obligation to buy anything."

This is kind of like how things go at the pool. We know as parents not to say "don't run." The human mind omits the "don't" and our kiddos hear,

62

"run!" What's the best way to get kids to stop running? We yell at the top of our lungs, "WALK SLOWLY!" They instantly slow down.

If you change the phrase to include "obligation" or "pressure" you run the risk of your potential customer only hearing that negative, icky word. I recommend sticking with "don't have to get anything." It's safer and more positive.

Trap #2: ONLY saying "you don't have to get anything."

Sometimes in our head we write a story that we are being high pressure or pushy when we ask someone if they want to order something. It's not true. This thought creates a feeling of fear that then leads to omitting the "if you see something you like, I'll help you order it today."

This is dangerous. Imagine someone comes to you, feebly sharing, "you don't have to get anything today. How does that sound?" You would agree. To not buy something that day. This salesperson just told you not to order. Confidence, belief and enthusiasm are contagious. So is a LACK of confidence, belief and enthusiasm.

If the salesperson is not confident enough to encourage you to get something, WHY WOULD YOU CONVINCE THEM?!?!?!!

This reminds me of a time I went to the hockey store a few years ago to get new roller hockey skates.

Roller hockey skates are heavy, and the last time I'd bought a pair was probably 12 years ago. Last year my grandma gave me a ton of birthday money out of the blue. I thought, "now is the time to splurge." (Perhaps I'm like most moms who don't tend to buy nice things for themselves.)

I had researched online and knew the best skates on the market were $600-$1,000. Now as you are reading this you might be thinking I'm crazy, as a middle-aged woman, to invest that much in roller hockey skates. But my shins hurt from a basketball injury in college, and I wanted to play better more than I wanted to save the gift money.

I went to what is known as one of the best hockey stores in Southern California. I walked confidently to the skates salesperson and said, "I'd like to get the lightest roller hockey skates you have."

He brings me some skates. I had my old ones with me, which were also very high quality from over a decade ago. I knew the technology would be better and today's skates would be lighter.

But it was a lot of money. I found some skates for $800 and $1,000. (I know). It was a lot of money and I wanted to be sure. "Can you go weigh the difference?"

He came back. "These are X grams lighter, and these are Y grams lighter."

I asked, "do you think it will matter?"

His response (as likely a young college student WITHOUT broken shins), "I think the ones you have are pretty good." I wasn't going to convince him that he was wrong and that it is a better idea for me to buy the new skates. That would be super weird and actually kind of embarrassing on my part. The expert just told me I don't need to get something. Who was I to question him?

I left without new skates. I was sad. I got home and Charlie asked where my new skates were. I didn't have any. He got super frustrated with me. My sweet, never confrontational husband scolded me, "go and get lighter skates, it will help."

So I went to the other hockey store in the area. I walked right in and bought $800 skates in seconds. I played in them the next day.

Charlie was right. (Oh no! It's in writing!) The new skates mattered. The first hockey skate sales guy UNSOLD ME. All he had to do was be confident. He didn't have to claim that it would help my shins, there was no way to know.

But he could have simply said, "These are the best skates on the market. You won't regret it, I think you should get them." I would have bought them, been happy and not had to admit to the whole world that my husband was right.

What's the moral of the story? Your CUSTOMER will have a better experience if you smile, look him/her in the eye and softly share, "You don't have to get anything, but if you see something you like, I'll help you order it today. How does that sound?"

Pro Tip

You can mix and match the lines in the agenda meant to remove pressure in a way that feels natural to you. The most important thing is that your phrase MUST include both the remove pressure, and the agreement to look for things to order.

Here are some more examples:

1.   If you want to get something, great! If not, no big deal. Is that fair?

2.   If you think it's a good fit, we will talk about steps to move forward. If not, that's totally ok. I just want to make sure you are making the most informed decision. How does that sound?

3.   At the end I'm going to share with you guys how to learn more about working with us if you think we can help you reach your goals. Either way, this is a free webinar, and we are glad you are here. (This is what I will say during my webinars for my coaching business.)

Remember that idea of the high pressure and pushy person you don't want to be? Have I taught you anything that is high pressure or pushy?

See, sales training isn't so bad, is it? *wink*

Customer First Takeaways

•   Your business will rely on your ability to create trust, show compassion, establish stability, and inspire hope. It starts within the first 60 seconds of your appointment.

•   **"Just to review, today we are going to go over your _____ goals, a little about the company, and the most popular kits. My part will take about 30 minutes. You don't have to get anything, but if you see something you like, I'll help you order it today. How does that sound?"**

•   Give your customers the "license to buy" early.

•   Be confident that your customer's life will be better if they choose to buy. Transfer this confidence with a smile and by making a simple agreement.

CHAPTER 8

DID YOU NOTICE MY HUGE BELLY?

Shortly after Charlie and I got married, we relocated from the Los Angeles area to Orange County where I grew up. We moved into a perfect (well… Charlie has other words for it) one-bedroom apartment in Costa Mesa, 10 minutes from my new office.

As I mentioned earlier, I don't love change. So yes, it was the same complex I lived in before I got transferred to Los Angeles.

After one terrifying miscarriage scare and a week of bedrest, we made it to the third trimester. The baby was showing, as was the fact that I had eaten all of the pizza in Costa Mesa. It was time to look for a two-bedroom place.

The first step was to meet with a leasing agent, and it was not a great experience. She quickly passed us off to someone else, as if she couldn't be bothered with this young couple.

I am very passionate about being a good human in sales (obviously), so this was strike one. Charlie could see my blood start to boil. I took a deep breath and we continued.

The complex had all the things. Gym, close to work, new buildings, etc. But I wasn't feeling it.

What happened?

There wasn't one question along the lines of:

1. Why are you looking into moving?

2. Is this your first child?

3. What kinds of things are important to you in finding a place to live?

It would have been so easy. I was an easy target. But she didn't ask us one question. And we didn't lease there.

Prove You Care

This leasing agent was telling her company's story. Owns X percent of properties, state of the art this and that, etc.

But do people buy because of the company's story?

People buy because of THEIR story. Yet most network marketers start with their own story. And what happens to the customer's face when the story isn't their own? You know it, that glazed-over look.

I'm not saying your story isn't important. It is. I'm just going to argue that we have an opportunity to put the customer's story FIRST and then share ours.

> *"People don't care how much you know until they know how much you care."*

> **-Teddy Roosevelt**

You have probably heard that one before. Remember that whole customer first, team second, ego third philosophy? Our ego wants to lead with our story. But this doesn't always serve the customer for a couple of reasons. First, they may not identify with your story. Second, it takes the mic away from them.

What is the most important topic of this sales conversation? THE CUSTOMER!

What is the most important topic of this sales conversation? THE CUSTOMER!

We have started with the agenda. We have given our agenda, now it's time for collaboration to complete the agenda. This way we will know

67

what to spend additional time explaining, and we can personalize the conversation for our customer.

> *"Just to review, today we are going to go over your _____ goals, a little about the company, and the most popular kits. My part will take about 30 minutes. You don't have to get anything, but if you see something you like, I'll help you order it today. How does that sound?"*
>
> *"What do you want to make sure we go over today?*
>
> *"I want to personalize this conversation to you. Tell me about your _____ goals for you, and your family."*
>
> *"What else?"*
>
> *"How will reaching those goals, or solving those problems, impact your overall quality of life?"*
>
> *"What else?"*
>
> *What do you already know about [company name]? Ok great, let me tell you a little bit about us.*

Let's break it down!

"What do you want to make sure we go over today?

We ask this because it's respectful. We want to build a collaborative agenda. We have just shared with our potential customer what WE want to cover. It's only fair to ask them what they want to cover. This also helps us to know what their biggest concerns might be, in the very beginning. We will be able to spend more time addressing this throughout the conversation.

A word of caution: do not start addressing these things right here. Write them down so they know you are paying attention, tell them you have them and will get to them, and keep moving.

"I want to personalize this conversation to you. Tell me about your _____ goals for you, and your family."

Do you want to bore them with information that they don't care about? Of course not! And they don't want to be bored with information. We want to personalize it and we need to just tell them that.

Many network marketers prefer even to just use, "I don't want to bore you with information. Tell me about your _____ goals for you and your family."

You may have noticed that I said, "you and your family." You don't want to just change the life of your potential customer—you also want to help the people they love the most.

Customers are more likely to buy products to help the ones they love than they are to buy products for themselves. They are more likely to remember to use the product when it's given to someone in their family. I'm a whole lot more likely to make my kids take their supplements than I am to take my own. It doesn't make sense, but it's true.

One critical mistake many network marketers make is that they are so afraid of the price that they fail to offer two packs of whatever is available: one for the customer and one for the spouse. This isn't a trick to "get more sales." I want you to honestly look at the use of your product in your household. I am betting

> *Customers are more likely to buy products to help the ones they love than they are to buy products for themselves.*

that you and your spouse both use your core product.

"What else?"

After you ask about their goals or problems, keep going. Customers typically have more goals than they first share.

Smile kindly and ask, "What else?" They answer. You write down what they said. "What else?" They answer and you write. The most important goals or problems will typically come up after 1-3 "what elses" when they have time to think. Don't rush them.

When you do this, it might feel a little awkward and a little tense. Let me explain why.

No one does it. When was the last time your spouse, best friend, or sister asked you about your day and then followed up with, "that's so interesting, what else?"

I'll bet that has rarely, if ever, happened to you, even though they love you very much.

What if we did it? What message would that send to that person? That we CARE.

I am sure you got into this business because you care about people and love people. THIS is where we prove it.

We need to love well by listening hard. I am sure you have heard that God gave us one mouth and two ears for a reason.

As your potential customer is sharing their goals or problems, you may be tempted to interject. You may be tempted to share that you also have suffered from that problem. You might enthusiastically want to blurt out that you can help with that.

> *We need to love well by listening hard.*

It's this well-meaning behavior that is actually perceived as salesy and pushy. It makes the conversation about you or your company instead of about them. The unintended result of this interruption is that they will tense up and have resistance to your solution.

Remember, "people don't care how much you know until they know how much you care."

"How will reaching those goals, or solving those problems, impact your overall quality of life?"

We think that people might want things, or money, or relief from a certain problem. But actually, they just want a "better" life. Everyone has a different definition of a better life. This question is also really awesome for potential business builders.

I remember doing a complimentary coaching call for the sweetest lady named Debbie and I asked her about her network marketing goals. First, she shared her income and rank goals with me. Next, I asked her, "How will reaching those goals impact your overall quality of life?"

The answer she gave was so moving. She shared that she would use the money to travel to her grandkids as much as possible. She was sad her kids lived all over the country and was very motivated to make sure she would not miss out on her grandkids' lives.

I watched her over the next several months reach new ranks, earn a car, and I saw so much joy in her eyes in all of her pictures.

There is a very popular adage, "People don't want a drill. They want a hole." They don't want the product in and of itself. They want the thing that the product creates.

This question continues to show your potential customer that you care about them more than the sale, which you do. This question moves you toward the role of "trusted advisor" and out of the role as "salesperson."

Now your job is to help them to find ways to have a better life, which is really cool.

"What do you already know about [company name]? Ok great, let me tell you a little bit about us."

Now, your customer is likely all talked out. It's time to transition the conversation to talk about solutions.

When you ask this question, they will tell you what they know or don't know. This is good information for you to write down. More often than not they will give an answer like, "really not that much" and they will lean forward, eager for you to bridge that knowledge gap.

> *The key to "customer first" sales is to find a problem that they want to solve.*

After this question, you will go over the basics of your company, product line, and what makes you different from other options out there.

As stated in the very beginning of this book, all business can be boiled down to this: find a problem, solve it, make a sale, get paid. Many people skip to the third part and ask, "how can I make a sale?" The key to "customer first" sales is to find a problem that they want to solve. Now you are on the same team, instead of having some weird win-lose relationship. Every purchase moving forward is a win-win toward a better life.

Customer First Takeaways

- The customer's problems and goals are the most important part of the conversation.

- "People don't care how much you know until they know how much you care." —Teddy Roosevelt

- Ask about their goals for them AND their family.

- Ask, "what else?" until they are done sharing to build maximum trust.

CHAPTER 9

UNSOLD AGAIN

The sales profession gets a bad rap because so many people link the whole profession to the infamous "car salesman." The last time I bought a new car was our minivan. I was seven months pregnant with our second child, Haley. My little sports car could only fit one car seat. I like to think I traded in my dream car (BMW 325i) for my dream life (too many car seats for a BMW 325i). I know, adorable right?

We had already done some research online. We knew we wanted a Mazda 5, so Charlie and I went to the local Mazda dealership. We walked up and it was "Jim's" turn in rotation.

Me: Hi, we want to look at the Mazda 5.

Jim: Ok, great. Do you want to take a test drive?

Me: Not really, what's the difference between the base model and the Grand Touring?

Friends, I kid you not. "Jim" said, "hold on, let me go look at the cars." He left to run around the parking lot to look at the STICKERS ON THE CARS and came back with a notepad on the differences.

While he was gone, I had already looked up the differences on my phone.

Me: What are the interest rates you have available?

Jim: I can't tell you that until you fill out an application.

Me: Let's just say I have perfect credit. What's the lowest that's available?

Jim: I won't know until you do an application.

Me: I just looked online, it's 0.9% over 5 years. Perfect.

We took a test drive and didn't buy the car. Jim tried to pin us down so we didn't leave. I was unimpressed. If you are going to sell me anything, at least know something about your products. I can look up the "information" myself. I need you to help me understand what I need and how it will help me to have a better life.

Don't worry, we got the car two days later. We called the fleet manager. He wanted to give half the commission to Jim. I was super annoyed that the person who literally UNSOLD US (see how this happens all the time) was going to get paid. I have issues with bad salespeople.

Some people unsell by knowing nothing, like "Jim." However, some people go to the other extreme by giving a comprehensive list of features for every product. This is done in hopes that something will stick in the customer's mind. However, the customer is bored when you are talking about things that don't relate to their life. I only care about one thing: how it's going to help me. When customers move into this "bored" state, you have lost your ability to provide a solution to their problem.

It's critical that we learn to speak our customers' language, and all they care about is benefits. If we speak in features, it's the same as if my mother-in-law spoke to me in Chinese. I would only know the bad words.

Features and benefits

Feature: a prominent part or characteristic

Benefit: something that produces good or helpful results or effects or that promotes well-being

Here is an example from our car situation, if Jim spoke my language.

Feature: The Grand Touring has a sunroof with X and Y dimensions. (Jim just pulled this off the sticker)

Benefit: The Grand Touring has a sunroof. Have you ever been driving around Southern California on a beautiful day? When you have this sunroof you will be able to open it, have the sun on your face and really take advantage of that high mortgage you pay. You will be so happy when the sunroof is open. How does that sound?

I want to be happy when I'm driving around and therefore I now want the sunroof! The sale is made and the happy customer is feeling super cool.

There are three ways to explain the benefits of a product.

1. Earlier you mentioned…

2. Have you ever…

3. You might not need to use this everyday, but you will be glad you have it when…

Earlier you mentioned…

This transition directly references the goals and problems your customer shared earlier. You will directly address their pain points and show how this particular product is an obvious solution.

Let's say Jim had asked a question like, "what's important to you when it comes to your next car?" I would have replied with something like, "I want it to be easy to get the kids out."

Jim: The Mazda 5 has two sliding doors. Earlier you mentioned you want to make sure you can get the kids out easily. You won't have to worry about hitting the car next to you and will have plenty of room to quickly get your kiddos out. How does that sound?

This is the simplest explanation of a product and its benefits, since the customer made it easy for you. However, not every product in your most popular kit is going to line up directly with the goals or problems. It's ok, because we are not only going to help them solve the problems they mentioned. We are going to help with more than that!

Have you ever…

With this transition, we will be able to bring up common scenarios that they have likely experienced. This will allow the customer to visualize the many ways they will use the products.

Jim: Have you ever had a hard time finding a parking spot while driving a minivan or SUV, or noticed that every open spot in the lot is "compact?"

Me: Yes.

Jim: The Mazda 5 has six seats only, making it the same width as all of the other Mazdas even though it's a minivan. This means that your Mazda 5 will fit in compact spots. With the sliding doors I mentioned earlier, it will be much easier to park. What do you think?

Me: I think that sounds awesome.

Use common scenarios that almost everyone has experienced and you are likely to get a positive head nod from your potential customer.

Now you have provided more value than the "information" they can find online. You have exposed a problem they FORGOT they had, and eliminated future frustration.

You might not need to use this everyday, but you will be glad you have it when…

You have explained products by connecting them to existing problems and common problems. Now it's time to highlight uncommon problems.

Jim: The Mazda 5 has six seats. You might not use all six everyday, but you will be glad you have them when you need to take your parents out to dinner, or when your kids have friends you need to take care of. This way you won't need to take two cars everywhere. How does that sound?

Me: Perfect!

Focus on scenarios where your potential customers will have positive benefits, instead of bullet points and "information." Share solutions to current, past, and future problems. Remember you are already established as a trusted advisor who will help improve their overall quality of life.

> *Use common scenarios that almost everyone has experienced and you are likely to get a positive head nod from your potential customer.*

By explaining scenarios, it's also much more likely your customer will take the product out of the box and actually use it!

Customer First Takeaways

•   Know the common scenarios where your customers will use each of your most popular products.

•   Explain each product with a scenario:

  ▫ "Earlier you mentioned…"

  ▫ "Have you ever…"

  ▫ "You might not need this every day, but you will be glad you have it when…"

•   Keep it simple and help your customer envision themselves using the products to solve the problems.

•   Write down three scenarios or uses for each product in your company's most popular kit and put them into a Google Doc so it's easy for your team to duplicate this highly effective technique with ease.

CHAPTER 10

MAKE IT EASY TO BUY

Remember Blockbuster Video? Oh boy, now you know how old I am. For those of you who don't remember a world before digital cameras, Blockbuster Video was the place you would go on the weekend to pick out a movie to watch with your friends and family.

I know! You had to leave the house to get a movie! Those were dark times.

Each week, the new releases would come out. Blockbuster was the best job for a college student because we got to see as many movies as we could for free!

The new releases were lined on the wall of the store. A popular new release like Pulp Fiction would get two full shelves and we would probably carry 300 copies of that one movie for rental. As time went on, we would sell the previously viewed copies until eventually the popularity waned to where we would only carry two or three of each movie.

Then the movie would go into "the library." "The library" was the middle of the floor where all the older comedies, dramas, action films, etc. lived for the rest of their time. There were hundreds of movies to choose from.

I noticed the same trend week after week. There were two categories of people. The first category would walk in the store and, with their head on a swivel, turn right toward the "new release board." They would quickly review the titles of the 2-3 movies released that week, go grab one, and out the door they went.

The second category hung out in the library. Perhaps they got there too late on Saturday night and the good new releases were gone. Or maybe they had a coupon that wouldn't work on new releases. For whatever reason, they ended up in "the library." This would seem like heaven, right? Hundreds of the best movies ever. Something curious would happen. They would look for what seemed like HOURS. Many people never even got something after shopping around for over 30 minutes.

I didn't realize what was going on until I learned this simple principle in sales: a confused mind doesn't buy.

It was easier for customers to decide from 2-3 choices of movies and they ended up happier because they moved into action with a decision. Trying to choose from hundreds of movies felt more agonizing, and customers left with nothing, or "ok I guess this one." They actually seemed LESS happy!

> *A confused mind doesn't buy.*

I now see myself engaging in the same movie watching behavior. There are so many choices of shows I COULD watch on Netflix, Hulu, Amazon, and Disney Plus. I have found myself spending almost as much time looking for something to watch as it would take me to watch it!

At the time I'm writing this, Charlie and I just finished watching Madam Secretary, which was amazing. Charlie and I have spent HOURS trying to figure out which show we should start watching. We finally picked one, and I'm totally having second thoughts the whole time while thinking that maybe we chose the wrong one. For a few weeks, we actually watched NOTHING because we couldn't make a decision.

Too many choices seems like a great idea, but is actually counterproductive to customer success.

Confusion Elimination

Let's walk through what we have already done in our "customer first" sales process.

You started by setting up an appointment where you explained to the potential customer exactly what you will cover, how long it will take, and he/she agreed. YES! Then you laid out the agenda, helping both of you feel comfortable. There is an agreement that if we find something that solves problems, the customer will consider buying that day. We learned about their goals and problems and the potential customer feels like you are an advocate for them. You have also quickly explained the product line so they understand why they would use the products, and understand scenarios that apply to their life.

Everything is going really well, and then you get to the end...

Now what? Most people really struggle with what to say at the "time to buy part."

One option is to shyly ask, "do you want to get something?"

A second option is to show them a catalog or handout with a ton of options and asking, "what would you like to get?"

Neither of these work all that well. What tends to happen is the customer's face glazes over again. They whisper those dreaded words, "I'd like to think about it."

Nooooooooooo..... what happened here?

A confused mind doesn't buy.

When a customer responds with "I'd like to think about it" in most cases it means something is hijacking their ability to be CONFIDENT in their decision. This is very similar to the "I need to talk to my spouse" response. They want to talk to their spouse because they aren't quite sure and they want to make the right decision.

As stated earlier, confidence, belief and enthusiasm are contagious. So is lack of confidence, belief and enthusiasm.

You have a perfect storm of lack of confidence. Your customer is new to your products so they are understandably unsure. You aren't very confident with the best options to share with them. The lack of confidence transfers back and forth between you and your customer very subtly.

As we walk through what most would consider the "closing section," we need to remember that our customer comes first, team second, and our ego comes third.

Instead of giving a catalog, or asking a question like "what do you want to get?" let's offer two simple choices instead.

It would be so much easier for a customer to answer the following question: **This is the complete kit and this is the starter kit. Which do you think would work better for your family?**

Does a potential customer need to "think about" if a complete kit or starter would be better for their family? Do they need to "talk to their spouse" if they know which one is in their price range?

Not usually. Offering two choices makes it really simple for your customer to move forward and take action. The best part is that they still get to choose. You can show them the two most complete options first. If neither work for them, show two more. If those don't work, show two more.

If you are wondering if this approach is pushy, it's not as long as you keep in mind that they are typically saying, "no thank you" just to THOSE options. It's really helpful to say something like, "No problem, let me show you a couple of options that might work better for you and your family. How does that sound?" Your customer will be happy that you are still advocating for their family, and their problem with not being able to afford something hasn't made things weird.

> *Offering two choices makes it really simple for your customer to move forward and take action.*

There are several common mistakes that network marketers make during the buying process.

Mistake #1: Offering Only Low Priced Options

This mistake occurs when the salesperson has issues around the affordability of the product, and/or really wants to avoid the discomfort of hearing "I can't afford it."

Remember how frustrated I got buying roller hockey skates? The next summer I decided it was time to upgrade my ice hockey skates.

I went to the store that finally had let me buy roller hockey skates and figured I'd have a much better experience. "Hi, I'd like the lightest, most comfortable skates you have please."

We then spent about 15 minutes trying on skates he brought out which I assumed were the best ones they had. I picked some and asked how much they would be.

Let's just say they were not the best skates, they were the "affordable ones."

I had been pre-judged. The salesperson seemed to be in his early 20s, and perhaps was still a college student. I was clearly a mom. He didn't know I had $1000 burning a hole in my pocket. He offered me the skates he would have started with.

I was not happy he gave me an "affordable" option. I was frustrated that I had to spend another 20 minutes trying on skates and that I wasn't offered the best product from the beginning.

Luckily, I am a sales coach and knew exactly what was happening here. I knew he was kind, well-meaning, and just trying to find me the right option. I know he wasn't trying to be offensive. He was trying to be helpful. However, his action had the opposite effect. I was offended, and it wasn't helpful.

I want to drive home that point for you. It doesn't matter if you are well-meaning. By making assumptions about what people will spend or want, you run the risk of frustrating them.

Instead, offer the two most transformational kits your company has. Instead of making the decision about what kits to offer based on what you can afford or what the customer before this one could afford, base your decision on which kit will give them the best results.

Simply offer a few other options if the customer can't afford the premier options, or if they aren't a good fit for their family,

Mistake #2: Overselling the Largest Kit

You: "This amazing kit is the best deal in the entire world!!!!!"

Them: "I can't afford it."

You: (in a sad, disappointed tone) "Well, here is this other smaller kit."

Them: "Maybe I'll wait until I can afford the other one."

You: "Ok…"

And now it's awkward.

I want you to imagine that you are shopping for a dress or suit for your anniversary. You go to a store like Nordstrom and see the outfit of your dreams. It's perfect. Then you look at the price tag. You can't afford it.

A "customer first" salesperson would come up to, see your disappointment and say, "Yes, that is a nice dress. But you know what? I have one over here that I think would look even better on you! And the best part is that with the lower price, you can save the extra money for your anniversary dinner!"

Customers are not happy when they can't afford something. Have you ever been happy when you see something that meets your goals and solves your problems and you have to admit you can't afford it? Of course not.

Instead, get more excited as you move to the next options. Make them feel comfortable getting the next option, not like a loser. Keep offering two options at a time until there aren't any options left. You can use the transition, "No problem, I totally get it. Would it be helpful if I showed you a few other options that might be a better fit for your family?"

Keep offering two options at a time until there aren't any options left.

Remember, confidence, belief and enthusiasm are contagious.

Mistake #3: Giving the Idea That They Can "Buy Whenever They Want"

Why this mistake happens: The potential customer wants to "buy later" perhaps because of one of the mistakes we already mentioned. The salesperson just says ok, and moves on.

This hurts the customer because the feelings and knowledge they have is fresh in their mind. Tomorrow, they will forget half of what you covered.

The next day, they will forget even more. Their memory will deplete every day, and by the time you talk, all of the positive feelings have gone away. All they remember is you, and the price. They aren't likely to make the best decision for themselves in this space.

We want to make sure they solve their problems as quickly as possible. Think about your product for a second. Do you wish you had waited longer to start? Or do you wish you would have started earlier?

There are three ways to avoid this challenge proactively. The first is back in the gain input section. The customer is recalling their own internal motivation to move forward quickly when they share the answer to how reaching the goals will increase their overall quality of life.

Second, offer an incentive to buy today instead of tomorrow. You see these everywhere in the terms of sales, fast action bonuses, or what I like to call a "first appointment special." Choose something simple and something that they would like. Be excited about the special. Recently, Charlie and I signed our dog Piper up for obedience training. The trainer simply said, "If you want to register Piper today, we can give you $100 off." Bravo dog trainer! Bravo!

Third, share when they will receive the product instead of emphasizing the buying. People don't love spending money, but they love getting stuff. Sometimes it's a little obstacle because of the lack of instant gratification of needing to order the product. When you order something on Amazon there is writing that lets you know when you will receive the product that motivates you to buy today. You can say something like, "If you order today, you will get our kit on Friday, just in time to start using it over the weekend. And I can give you (first appointment bonus) as well. Would you like to go ahead and order it today?"

Mistake #4: Starting With the Lowest Priced Option.

Why this mistake happens: The network marketer wants to avoid an "I can't afford it." It may seem like a good idea to start at the bottom and add, but it actually is a higher difficulty level, and more awkward.

Potential customers typically will say no to the first offer. If they say no to your lowest-priced offer, there are no other options to show them. Start with the most complete kit first, and then give options two at a time until you find something they feel is a good fit. They will likely have better overall results, and your business will be more successful.

Remember, confidence, belief and enthusiasm are contagious. The buying part is FUN and your customer is counting on you to be the guide and the expert. Make their buying experience easy by offering two choices, and then two more until they find something that's a good fit for them.

Customer First Takeaways

- Make it simple to buy with a choice of two of your best, most comprehensive options.

- If those aren't a good fit, offer two more but keep your enthusiasm high.

- Offer a special or share the shipping date to keep customers excited about ordering sooner rather than later.

Confidence, belief, and enthusiasm are contagious. Keep these emotions high from the beginning to the end of your conversation.

SECTION 3

CUSTOMER FIRST LEADERSHIP

CHAPTER 11

IT'S ALWAYS WORTH IT

I will never forget the first time I coached a network marketing leader on recruiting. She is one of the best humans I have known since starting my coaching practice. She achieved a 6-figure income in her first full year in this particular company. Her motivation was to build a school in Africa, which she did.

She asked me to help her with recruiting. I really wasn't sure where to start, so I asked her to recruit me.

Me: I want to learn about the business, what would you say to me?

Her: It's really hard, but someday it will be worth it.

Me: Ummm….

We both laughed hysterically. Yes, achieving all of your major life goals is hard, and it's definitely worth it. We just needed a better pick-up line.

There is a difference between STARTING a network marketing business, and growing ANY business to a 6-figure income.

Even the most successful people in the business wish they were further ahead than they currently are. If you have been in business any amount of time, it's likely that it feels hard because business is all about trying new things.

I want to remind you that THIS IS OK.

The big question we need to ask is this: does "recruiting" belong in a book about putting customers first?

One hundred percent yes. A good thing you can do for your customers is to reach out to them, get to know them, and invite them to some sort of appointment so they can solve their problems. A better thing is to offer to help the people they care about.

An even better gift to your customer is to raise up additional leaders in communities throughout the world, so there are more people to serve customers.

We have already established that you believe in the life-changing properties of your product. Would you like to help five families per month, or 500? Or 5,000?

My daughter's midday anxiety ridden meltdowns are almost eliminated because a leader who lived 30 minutes from me believed in recruiting.

My rash from hell, caused by a wicked combo of overwhelm, auto-immune issues, and gluten sensitivity is all but gone because a company believed in getting the word out about its life-changing products.

I was not enrolled by the corporation, or their first distributor. I was enrolled, and helped because several people were focused and brave enough to invite people to see if they would like to start a business selling these particular products.

When I think about these two experiences, I think it's interesting that my life is better even though I wasn't enrolled by what the company would refer to as a "superstar." However, they are superstars in my life.

Repeat after me: recruiting is something you do FOR customers, not something you do TO customers.

Recruiting is something you do FOR customers, not something you do TO customers.

Offering someone a chance to earn some extra money on the side or to replace their career is a gift. The fact that they would be working with a product that helps people, and would have independence and an opportunity to constantly grow, is a gift.

Our customers benefit so much when we are enthusiastic and confident recruiters.

Benefit #1: More Customers are Reached

One person can only reach so many people. We need a team to help all the people. Customers may never hear about the products from someone they trust if we are doing this alone.

Benefit #2: When Customers Get Involved, They Retain Longer

Customer retention increases when their friends and family are also using the products. When I see my friends using the products, I use more products because it's top of mind. I also want to look cool around my friends by using the same thing they are using. Even if I don't stay as a committed builder, and you help me just enroll a few friends and family, everyone is better off.

Benefit #3: Different People Jive with Different People

Everyone has their own "tribe." Some people really connect with others because they live in the same state. Others connect because their kids are a similar age. Many of my clients connect with me because I love tacos. I totally get that not everyone connects with a taco-eating, hoodie-wearing business coach. This is why it's really great that I have a kale-eating, leather earring–wearing business partner.

Benefit #4: More Social Proof and Knowledge

Your story will impact some people. Your team members' stories will impact different people. The more people you have on your team, the more knowledge and success stories get passed around. This increased collaboration helps customers be more knowledgeable and confident, further increasing their ability to be successful with the products.

Benefit #5: More Service

I have had clients who literally enroll dozens of customers themselves each month. This is where they focus all of their attention. One of the problems they experience is they aren't able to give enough attention to the customers they have. By recruiting more business builders, the customer service work gets spread out and becomes more manageable for everyone.

What is recruiting?

The word "recruiting" can have a similar negative stigma as "sales." This is often because it's thrown around as something you should do to reach your goals, versus giving a gift of opportunity to those around you. Let's ground ourselves in the actual definition.

Let's go back to our good friend Merriam-Webster. To recruit in the network marketing context means to fill up the number with new members, or seek to enroll. I have seen other sources that give a definition of "enlist someone toward a cause."

Recruiting is inclusive in nature. As soon as I have someone tell me, "I just need to find one committed builder," I know they are stuck at a certain income level in their business.

Recruiting isn't about finding the one, it's about inviting the many, and "the one" emerging. In *Rock Your Network Marketing Business*, Sarah Robbins shares that most million-dollar earners have recruited between 50 and 100 builders, and 80% of their income comes from 3-5 of them.

Recruiting isn't about finding the one, it's about inviting the many, and "the one" emerging.

The job of a network marketing leader is to invite people to learn about how they can also earn money by starting their own business. Next, their role is to educate them on how it works. If the person moves forward, the role of the leader is to work with them to get started. The most committed will be mentored or invited to professional development events.

91

It is your job to invite EVERYONE to explore, whether or not you think they would all be successful. Their success is not your decision.

> *"If you are standing with other women in a circle and there is a woman standing alone in your circle's vicinity—the thing to do is to notice her, smile at her, move over a bit and say, "Hi, come join us!" Even if she decides not to join your circle— even if she looks at you like you're crazy—inviting her is STILL THE THING TO DO. This advice is meant for both literal and figurative circles. WIDEN YOUR CIRCLE. ALL THE TIME."*

—Glennon Doyle

This is not a network marketing quote. This is a life quote. The bigger your circle is in life, the more influence you have. The more influence you have, the more impact you will have. It's really that simple.

I look at recruiting kind of like an Indian wedding. If you haven't been to an Indian wedding, I'll explain. Weddings are INCLUSIVE, not exclusive. We invite everyone who is important to us. If they live in a different state, or different country, it doesn't matter. They are invited. It is up to them if they choose to come. We will not make that decision for them. It's important for everyone to know that even if it's not likely that they come, they are still invited, welcome, and loved. If they change their mind later, we will figure out a way to make it work.

The invitations are for the whole family. It's a place for everyone to get involved. Everyone is welcome.

As with any wedding, there are many roles. There are the bridesmaids who are there early, and stay late. They are the most involved. On the other side of the spectrum are those who come for cocktail hour and head out early.

It's my job to invite, and it's their job to decide if they will attend, and how involved they will be. It's also worth mentioning that I'm not in contact with everyone who attended my wedding. But I'm glad they came and they are too. It's still a positive experience even if we aren't best friends to this day.

This is the same in network marketing. Our job is to encourage, support skill development, and give clarity to the best of our abilities. Their job is to work. If they get a little out of the experience, great. If they have a full-time business, that's great too.

Our job is to invite, their job is to decide. Period.

We can just keep it simple, tell them the truth, and invite them to learn more.

> *"I don't want to make any assumptions—would you like to learn how to earn money with [company name]?"*

They can respond with yes, no, maybe, or it depends. Either way, you have done your job to widen your circle. You can sleep well at night knowing you are doing a good job. You might be thinking right now, "ok I'm in, but how do I implement this?"

Invitation Opportunity #1: Direct Invitation to Someone Who Doesn't Know About the Products

"I wanted to reach out to you because I was thinking about you today. I am starting/doing a business working with (product) to help people with (goal/problem). I don't want to make any assumptions—would you like to learn how to earn money with this company as well?"

Invitation Opportunity #2: When a Customer Enrolls or Purchases Retail

"Your product will arrive in a few days. I don't want to make any assumptions—would you like to learn how to earn money with [company name?]"

Invitation Opportunity #3: Wishlist Appointments

We recommend that our clients have second appointments with customers to create a wishlist, show them how to order, get the best value, etc. This is also a great opportunity for an invitation to learn more.

"Most people want to know how the earning money part works, even if just out of curiosity. Is that kind of the same for you?"

Invitation Opportunity #4: Customer Care Outreach

"I just realized that I don't think I've ever actually asked you, and I'm sorry. I don't want to make any assumptions—would you like to learn how to earn money with [company name]?"

Or...

"I know I have asked you before, and I like to check in from time to time because I know things change for families sometimes. Feel free to say 'no thanks,' I won't be upset. Would you like to explore how to earn money with [company name]?"

If they say yes or maybe...

"Great! Why do you think this might be important to you? How could (their answer) impact your overall quality of life?"

"Awesome, I'd be glad to help you. Usually what I do is set up a time to go over how this would help you and your family, what you would do, how compensation works, and what the next steps would be. My part would take about 45 minutes and then of course whatever questions you have. If you want to move forward, cool. If not, no big deal. Either way, I want to make sure you make the most informed decision. How does that sound?"

Remember, inviting people to learn more about the business is something we do FOR customers, not something we do TO them. If we put customers first and consistently serve them, they will be more connected to us and our company. There are more opportunities for you to invite and for them to opt-in to be a builder.

But if they buy once randomly and never again, or never hear from you, it's not very likely they are going to just start a business out of the blue. Just widen your circle, friend. You will figure it out along the way. Once you invite them to an appointment, adapt the rest of the five keys you learned earlier to make recruiting an enjoyable process for you and your customers. Hooray!

Customer First Takeaways

• Recruiting is something you do FOR customers, not TO customers.

• Widen your circle—inviting is the right thing to do.

• You have an ethical obligation to invite people to learn about the business, and it doesn't have to be weird.

• Our job is to invite to an appointment, their job is to make the decision to attend an appointment and possibly start their own business.

• Once you invite people to learn more about the business, use the five keys to make recruiting an enjoyable process for you and your customer.

CHAPTER 12

PROGRAM YOUR GPS

You may have heard the term "vision" come up every once in a while at professional development events. Leaders will encourage you to "tell people your vision," and you don't know what that even means or how to do it. Sometimes you try and brilliance comes out of your mouth, and sometimes you try and the person you are speaking with stares back blankly.

Your vision is the mental picture you have in your head about what your business will look like in the future.

Vision is critical because it determines your path, determines your strategy, and helps you to focus. If you know where you are going and are excited about it, you are less likely to get distracted by obstacles.

> *Your vision is the mental picture you have in your head about what your business will look like in the future.*

Your life is going to operate much like a GPS. You can't just tell your phone, "go somewhere cool." You have to decide where you want to go. You put in the destination, and your GPS will start to build you a path. If you make a detour or hit traffic, your GPS will still get you there, eventually.

We still need to determine a destination. If we want other people to meet us at this destination, we need to tell them where we are going too. Based on where they live, they might take a different route. They may join you for the whole excursion, or stop in for a bit. They might want to drive with you. Everyone will have different commitment levels. They might even say they can't or don't want to go, but they might come next time.

No matter what, EVERYONE needs to know where you are going. Now you might be panicking, "Tasha, I don't even know where to start." That's ok, I got you.

It will take a lifetime for you to figure out what you really want from life and from your business. It will change.

One thing that will not change is that **you are creating a team of people who help others with their _____.**

This is the job of the network marketing leader. Your job is to create the largest team of people who help other people. The end. This vision also doubles as an excellent guiding star for you, your team, and your customers.

> **Example 1: We are creating a team of people who help others with their health.**
>
> **Example 2: We are creating a team of people who help others with their confidence.**
>
> **Example 3: We are creating a team of people who help others with their financial security.**

Imagine for a second that I challenged you to go door-to-door. I'm not actually asking you to do this, just imagine it. Let's say you had 10 people open the door and you simply said, "Hi, I'm [your name here] and I live up the road. I'm creating a team of people who help others with their health. Would you like to be involved?"

How many do you think would say, "sure" or "it depends what it is?" I doubt people would slam the door rudely in your face. A few might say "no thanks."

I think at least half would have a positive response. My point is not to go door-to-door, although it is your business and you can if you want. My point is that this vision is super attractive.

Let's break down why this vision works so well.

"I'm creating a team of people that help others with their _____."

Reason #1: We are Born to Create

As kids, we loved building blocks. We would play with our food and build towers instead of eating it. Our children go to the bathroom and run out saying, "MOMMY! Look what I made!" We keep IKEA furniture longer because we made it. We spend $50 for a plate at Color Me Mine because we painted pottery ourselves.

Creating is fun, it's messy and it's infinite.

Reason #2: It's Simple and Everyone Can Understand It

If you are speaking, and they don't understand, are you communicating? If a 4th grader can't understand it, we probably shouldn't say it. This vision is clear enough for a 4th grader to understand, which means your customers and team members will also understand! In your home, where you work, it's likely that you have a much more detailed vision for what you want your business to look like. I call this the "inward facing vision." It's for you, to get you excited and help with a plan. The simple vision I am teaching you here is your "outward facing vision." It's one that everyone can remember and be a part of.

Reason #3: You Can Sneak It In Everywhere

It's a simple sentence, but the more you say it, the more everyone believes it and will work toward this team. Every time you say it, you will also hear it! The person you need to convince the most is yourself.

It's simple to share during sales conversations, recruiting conversations, team meetings, recognition of builders, and even when your friend from yoga asks you how things are going with that little business of yours.

Reason #4: People Want to Be a Part of Something That is Going Somewhere

Which business do you think a customer would want to be a part of?

One where the business owner wasn't sure if they were going to be around in a few months?

Or one where they are creating a team of people dedicated to helping others with an important goal or problem?

Obviously, the latter. Whether they join your team as a builder or not, they are more likely to be drawn and loyal to you. Remember, people want trust, compassion, stability, and hope. They will know why you are doing what you are doing (trust), that you care about people (compassion), that you are in it for the long-term (stability), and there is a place for them (hope).

Attraction is Intentional

My mom has a few sayings that are ingrained in my soul. One is "life sucks, and then you die." The other is "would you rather be right, or happy?" The first was a response to complaining. It sounds negative but it's not. It simply means that life owes you nothing and so it's no good to complain about it. The second is pretty obvious why a mother would say this over and over to a young, arrogant kid with a strong sense of justice, fairness and what is "right."

When I repeat these sayings, I roll my eyes, but they have settled in. They are a part of who I am. To get this kind of message to be a part of me, how many times do you think my mom has repeated these exact words? Thousands of times, I'm sure. And now here they are, benefiting you!

Our vision needs to be repeated enough that it's in their soul.

Our vision needs to be repeated enough that it's in their soul. The day you get tired of saying your vision is the day your team only STARTS to hear it.

Vision is not an announcement at a team meeting. "Hey guys, by the way, last announcement. We are creating a team of people who help others with their _____. Have a great day!" And then it's over and never to be heard again. We need to share it so often that it becomes us.

Vision Opportunity #1: Your Sales Appointment

First, share the agenda. Second, gain input.

Third, you are actually going to share a little about your company and THIS is where I think the best place to go into your story is.

"What makes [company] different is...I'd like to briefly share with you why I decided to do this as a business." Share a product testimonial, if applicable, and now it's time to share our vision.

"So now I'm creating a team of people who help others with _____. If you would like to learn more about how to earn money doing this as well, let me know afterwards and we can set up a time to chat in more detail. But for now, let's focus on the products."

Vision Opportunity #2: Team Communication

We want to communicate our vision consistently to our team as well. We can do this when we recognize people in a simple text, or at team events. Below are a few examples.

"I just want to let you know that I'm so glad to be working with you because (character trait). This is awesome because together we are creating a team of people that help others with their_____. I appreciate you."

"I am so glad you are all here at the team meeting today. Together, we are creating a team of people who help others with _____."

Vision Opportunity #3: Conversations With Friends/ Family

Have you ever been a little frozen when someone asks you how your business is going? I am. It's good because I'm helping people, but I'm still not exactly where I would love to be in order to shout from the mountain tops. Instead of giving them a status on our goals, we can share the vision and a win we are excited about. It's easy, true, and who knows—maybe they will catch the vision!

"Things are good! I'm excited because [success story]. This is cool because I'm creating a team of people who are helping others with their _____ so this makes me happy. Thanks for asking."

Our vision is our guiding star. It is truer than our current day circumstances, and it is our future. If we want a team of people that is impactful throughout the world, we must speak it into existence. Our vision will wake us up, it will wake up the superstars in our network, and it will wake up your team. And it's a lot more fun building a business when everyone is awake.

Customer First Takeaways

- A vision is a picture of the future of your business, and a declaration of what you are creating.

- Your vision can be as simple as, "I am creating a team of people who help others with their _____."

- The purpose of your vision is to create a team who creates customers.

- The most important person to hear your vision constantly is yourself.

- Share your vision in appointments, meetings and in everyday conversations.

CHAPTER 13

WHAT WE CAN LEARN FROM A DESK

I am not a master furniture builder. I haven't gone to any woodworking school. I don't even have a proper drill that can make a hole anywhere.

But in our home, I have made a bed, two kids desks, three cabinets, and the desk that I'm using as I'm typing this paragraph right now. None of the desks have tipped over, the cabinets haven't broken, and no one has fallen through the bed.

Everyone who has used any of these items I have built has had an amazing sleeping, working, or storing experience. What's even more interesting is that my kids wouldn't say, "Mom made me the most amazing desk in the world" and gush on and on. They would say, "I love my desk." Wait, the desk gets the credit? Not the deskmaker?

How can all of this be? It's because Ikea gave me a written manual that I can reference when I'm building so I know what to do. The instructions are simple and only include how to build the item that I bought. The bed instructions don't also come with desk instructions, just in case. If I really need the desk instructions, I can go online and get them. I have only what I really need so I don't get overwhelmed.

The lesson here is that a manual is the key to a novice providing the customer (or in my case the furniture user) a great experience.

When I tell people I used to sell Cutco knives, I get one of a few predictable responses. One response is that they haven't heard of them. Poor things, their friends didn't refer them. I wonder why? Another response is that they say that they love their knives and loved how the scissors cut the penny. If the conversation goes a bit further they will say, "It was my (insert relationship here) who sold them to me and he/she did such a great job."

How did college students, students with no experience, conduct sales appointments BY THEMSELVES without a hitch? What's even more interesting is that I have never heard, "OH. MY. GOSH. Cutco? That's one of those scams right? The rep was so high pressure and pushy."

I am a rule follower and can be awkward when I don't know what to say. This is one of the main reasons Cutco is going strong since its inception in 1949. The product was able to shine because our directions were: cut rope, smile, and follow the manual.

This kind of "duplication" (that's the direct sales word for this) is possible because a manual and a bit of practice went a long way. I'm sure you have heard that word being thrown around and explained as the key to your entire business. You have heard, "It's not what works, it's what duplicates." You might be wondering how you go about with this mystical spell that you must cast on your downline to duplicate. The easiest way to duplicate is to simply take a day and write down what you say so they can do/say it too.

I personally have ZERO intuitive sales skills. I read from the manual and for many years had no idea what to say when a curveball was thrown at me. However, here I am, running a sales training company and writing a sales book anyway. I started as initially unqualified, and that helped me to be eventually qualified.

The easiest way to duplicate is to simply take a day and write down what you say so they can do/say it too.

Now I have a hard, real-deal question for you. Do you, as the leader of your business, have something like this for new builders? As I look back on my sales career I know one thing for sure: without the training manual, I would have failed.

Don't be salty right now toward your company or upline because they didn't give you a training manual with all the words. YOU are the CEO of your business. If I have convinced you that a manual for people getting started is important, then make one. As Mom would say, "Would you rather be right, or happy?"

What is the training manual?

The training manual is a document that has everything your new builders need to be successful in their first few weeks. It's goal is to provide worksheets and outlines for them to use to get their first 10 customers, first builder, and first 25 referrals.

I recommend you include the following in your completed documents:

- Your vision

- A place to brainstorm contacts

- A blank schedule to fill in with time management

- An overview of what they need to know about the products in the most popular kit

- How to invite people to a group event or a 1-on-1

- An outline of what to say at a group event or 1-on-1

- An outline of what to say in a 1-on-1 for a potential business builder

You don't have to wait until it's perfect to share this with your new builders. Right now, if you are like 99% of network marketers, you don't have anything in writing. You can easily record yourself in a conversation, play it back, and type it out. If you did one conversation per week, your manual will be done in a month.

The problem with not having a manual is that your team operates like a game of telephone. This is why duplication breaks down at level three for most leaders, even the good ones.

Many top leaders are intuitively good at connecting, influencing, and moving people into action. They either learned it somewhere else, or they have some natural talent.

At their best, most leaders are "winging it" and getting great results. If that's you, good job! This DOES NOT mean you will get great duplication. Your new builder watches you, over and over again. You may have a good student who takes tedious notes and practices in the mirror at home. However, it's more likely that you have someone who takes some notes and does their best, but their notes are incomplete. The leader is winging it. The new builder is now winging a "winged version." It still might get some results. But what about their own builder? They are winging the winged version of a winged version.

The core message that you were so good at delivering has become completely distorted, incomplete, and a novice has filled in the blanks with his or her lack of experience. Your whole team is operating like a game of telephone, and we know how that ends.

How do you fix the problems in a game of telephone?

You pass a note.

If I haven't convinced you yet, I have 10 reasons why the manual is the key to serving thousands of customers, having more joy and income in your business.

Reason #1: If You Don't Have a Manual, You are Playing a Game of Telephone

Your "earlier you mentioned you want to sleep better, this will help with that" becomes "if you have sleep apnea this will cure it like it did for my cousin" and you have a big problem. People get confused by the messages. If the messages are incomplete, your team goes into analysis paralysis. They don't act and, therefore, don't get results.

Reason #2: This Decreases Overwhelm for Your New Builder

"Welcome to the team! I want you to join these three Facebook groups, follow these four leaders on Instagram, attend the weekly company call,

105

and the weekly team call. I also recommend you get this great book called "Customer First—" it changed my life. And don't forget to write down your why and make your list of 100. Does that sound good? Ok great, talk to you later!"

How would you feel if you were greeted with this as a new builder? Overwhelmed, right? Overwhelmed people don't move into action. Just like with babies, limit their exposure until they are strong. Have them focus solely on getting their first 10 sales, so they have a strong foundation, before doing additional learning.

Reason #3: It Decreases Overwhelm for You

Let's be real. Part of the problem going to the next level in your business is because the idea of a new builder saying "yes" to joining you makes you want to hide under a blanket.

I call it the "what if they say yes" bottleneck, and all leaders have it. If you are starting out, you literally have no clue what to say or do. If you make around $5,000 a month you are starting to get really stretched for time and the thought of walking someone through every detail makes your heart race. And if you make $20,000 or more per month, you literally can't even with a new person.

Having all of your outlines written out is a major timesaver. It doesn't mean that every person will magically reach all of their goals, but at least you don't have to go through every word with them as they try.

Reason #4: It's a "Legacy" Document

Your training manual can be passed down to multiple generations in your business, even if some of your leaders make a few adjustments. This allows for duplication much further down on your team than if you had to communicate verbally.

Can you imagine living in a world where there were no books? What if you had to go to church to hear wisdom from the Bible? Messages would be distorted and there would be a lack of empowerment for all.

Reason #5: Google Docs

You can put your manual into a Google Doc so it's easy to share amongst your team. You and your team members can have the app on your phone so if you need to do some impromptu inviting, selling, or recruiting, they can just pull it up without a hitch!

Reason #6: You Don't Have to Always Be There

Three-way calls (conference calls with you as the upline, your team member, and their potential customer or builder) are a great tool and many people have been incredibly successful with them.

The problem is that they require everyone to be on the same schedule. If you are really good at your business, you will have a full schedule. If you have a manual, you might only need to do a couple of three-way calls and your builders will be able to do appointments themselves if you aren't available.

Remember that friend I had who said that the network marketing industry didn't need sales training? Her major rationale is that she is very successful because her upline did three-way calls with/for her for nine months as she learned. NINE MONTHS! Oy vey. I'm sure most of us cringe at the thought of training a new builder for nine whole months.

Reason #7: It Increases the Interest of Customers Building the Business

One of the main triggers for people to want to do the business is that they think it's simple and they can do it. When you have a manual that you or your builder are referencing, it increases confidence in the POTENTIAL builder.

When you have a manual that you or your builder are referencing, it increases confidence in the POTENTIAL builder.

If they see you using notes, they will believe all they have to do is refer to the notes and they won't need to be an expert. They are more likely to believe they can do it.

107

Reason #8: Saves Time

It will take a day to put together. Or you could spend three days training every new builder. Or you could be frustrated for four years with your new builders not launching or doing well. You choose…

With the outlines all in place, you can jump straight to answering questions, making adjustments, or practicing. You don't need to wait while your newbie tells you to slow down so he can write down what you just said.

Reason #9: Introverts Will Be Successful

Introverts like to know what they are going to do and say. They feel more comfortable when they are prepared and have practiced. Introverts are less likely to be able to improvise on the spot without panicking. Without structure and a plan of what to say, they are likely to clam up and feel like the business isn't for them.

My very first client went from making $50 a month to $450 a month because she had outlines she could practice. If she can do it, so can your introverted friends (or yourself). Your introvert won't have to worry about what he/she is going to say next—he/she will be able to use listening skills to connect and help more people.

Reason #10: Extroverts Won't Burn Through Their Contacts

In stark contrast, your extroverts will just go "talk to people." That's great! They are moving into action! But that doesn't mean what they are saying is right, effective, and lead to customers solving their problems. Give your extroverts a high-converting outline, and help them be more successful.

*Some people are true introverts and draw their energy from being alone. Some people are true extroverts and draw their energy from being around others. Most are like me. I am an ambivert and I'm somewhere in the middle. I exhibit aspects of both sides of the spectrum. The ambiverts will truly thrive with a manual.

What's included in the manual?

Warning: DO NOT make a comprehensive manual that has every single thing they will ever need to know. This will overwhelm you as you go to make it, and will overwhelm your builder that they need to know everything before they do any work. Complicating the manual is great for your ego, but not good for your customers as your team member stumbles and overthinks everything. Keep it as simple as possible to help them in their first few weeks. Once they get 10 sales, they can invest time and money into further professional development. All you are trying to do is give them a foundation.

Download a template at: customerfirstbook. com/training

If it's helpful, you can download a template at: customerfirstbook.com/training

Section 1: Welcome

Start your manual with a note that includes your vision and where to go with questions. Their first goal is to get their first sale. The second goal will be to find their first builder. The third goal will be to reach their 10th sale. If you want, you can create a little checklist. But please, please, look at it through the lens of a new person and don't overwhelm them.

Section 2: Contact List

Create a space where they can brainstorm who they want to contact first for appointments. They only need enough space to brainstorm for their first 15-25 meetings. It doesn't have to be several pages. One page with some lines and a short explanation will be perfect.

Section 3: A Printed Weekly Schedule for Their First Two Weeks

You can do a quick Google search to find one and include it. This will help with time management. Most people struggle with time management and figuring out how to fit in a business with the rest of their life. On this schedule, they can write in all of their commitments so they are able to clearly see when they have time to work.

Section 4: Outlines of How to Invite

They will likely need three short outlines. First, they will need an outline of what to say to invite someone to an event that you are facilitating. This will only be applicable if this is part of your process for starting people. Second, they will need an outline of how to invite someone to a 1-on-1 they will do themselves. Third, they will need an invitation to an event that they are facilitating.

Feel free to use what you are learning in this book about appointment setting as the framework for your invitations.

Section 5: Outline of Sales Conversation

The sales conversation is the appointment for a potential customer. Use the keys you learned earlier in this book as a guide for you. You may want to include two versions: one for the 1-on-1 and one for the group appointment. They need to be adjusted at the close and we don't want your new person to get stuck.

Section 6: Outline of Recruiting Conversation

You will want to include an outline for your builder to use if someone is interested in the business. When they just start, you may use a three-way call for this. However, your builder might not have that option and we want to empower them.

If you aren't sure what you actually say when you meet with someone about the business, just do a practice appointment and record yourself. You can play it back and type out what you are saying. Don't let this intimidate you. Do your best and work it out over time.

Section 7: Screenshots

You may want to include some screenshots on how they need to navigate the back office to enroll a customer or builder. This will help them not feel silly when they go to do it the first time.

Tips to Making This Work

1. Practice a few times with your builder to further increase confidence. Ask questions like, "does this sound like you?" or "Is there anything on here you want to adjust?" If it doesn't sound like them, they won't use it. Don't let your ego of it being perfect get in the way of action.

2. Use Google Docs to keep this document accessible to anyone, anywhere.

3. Don't wait until it's perfect. Start with the first couple of sections. A lot of people have gone over a decade without a recruiting conversation outline. Your builder will be ok until you sort it.

4. Gain agreement with your builder when you give it to them to increase the probability they will actually use it. Ask, "If I gave you all the outlines I use for my business, would that be helpful?"

5. Adjust it as time goes on. This will be your first draft. You will need to adjust based on new company information, experience, skill, etc. It's not etched in stone, and that's a good thing.

6. Only give them what they need for the first two weeks. You actually want them asking you questions so you stay connected in the first few weeks. They aren't ready to be totally independent yet. They need your connection and encouragement.

Only give them what they need for the first two weeks.

7. If you are more on the extroverted side like I am, just grind it out and don't be a wimp. I get it—I'd much rather be talking to someone right now instead of writing this book. But like you, I need

something that spreads my ideas even when I'm not talking. Give yourself a reward for finishing it or meet up with a friend and do it together. I promise, you will be so much more effective when you are talking to people, and it will be worth it.

8. Did you notice I haven't used the word "script" at all? People dislike scripts and don't want to feel "scripted." Most have had experience interacting with someone who used a script poorly and without judgement. We are giving them an OUTLINE so they can adjust based on the way they speak. My Southern California English won't work very well for someone who is born and raised in Massachusetts, or vice versa.

Grow your team by empowering your builders to serve customers well, from the beginning. The term empower means to give people the power. In a profession where we are paid to talk (and listen), give them the words to help them be successful. Forcing your builder to go through the school of hard knocks instead of sharing a training manual with him or her means that many families will not have the life- changing power of your products. It's worth a couple of days of typing for our mission.

> *Grow your team by empowering your builders to serve customers well, from the beginning.*

Customer First Takeaways

- Duplication takes sitting down and doing the work—it's ok, we can do hard things.

- Instruction manuals on what to do AND say help to increase confidence and results.

- Winging it may work for you, but won't serve your team.

- Having a manual saves time and decreases frustration and overwhelm.

- "Something" is better than "perfect".

- Download a template to make this easier at: <u>customerfirstbook.com/training</u>

CHAPTER 14

THEY WILL LEARN IT BY WATCHING YOU

I was born in the 1980s, back in the days where there were commercials. One commercial showed a high school boy sitting on his bed, happily listening to his headphones. His dad, with a full mustache and a maroon tie walks in the room with a box of drugs.

Dad: This yours?

Kid: No?

Dad: Your mother said she found it in your closet.

Kid: I don't know where it came from.

Dad: Tell me the truth!

Kid: Look, Dad—it's not mine!

Dad: Where did you get it?

Kid: Dad! It's...

Dad: Answer me! Who taught you how to do this crap?

Kid: You, alright? I learned it from watching you!

It ended dramatically with, "Parents who do drugs have children who do drugs."

The commercial was bad, and research shows that the anti-drug commercials did not reduce drug use. But it brings light to a very important point in parenting, and leadership: they learn it by watching us.

The undertone in that commercial is that the father is TELLING the kid what to do, but his actions are saying something different.

If you are a parent, you know this too, even though it's a hard thing to live on a daily basis. Our children will learn more by watching how we live than what they learn from our advice, instruction, nagging, or shame tactics.

Why would leadership be any different?

As leaders, we want our team to enroll customers, reach ranks, and be consistent. Many leaders move into "management mode" where they stop enrolling customers. Their focus shifts to their team, and away from their customers.

Things then start to get tense. Leadership shifts from, "let's do this together" to "do what I say, not what I do." Leaders try to work with their people to enroll customers. Their coaching skills are underdeveloped or nonexistent. It's not something they have ever been trained to do—coach people to sell stuff.

The leader starts to get discouraged. Volume starts going down. The leader feels no longer in control as he/she is trying to work with team members to make sales. Joy is sucked out of the business. People start getting stuck where there used to be so much hope.

If you have seen this in your business, you aren't alone. If you haven't been there yet, take the advice in the chapter and commit to never going there.

Do you want to have a team of people who get out of their comfort zone to enroll and retain customers? If yes, then clearly understand this: they will follow your lead.

Do you focus on customers and engage in activities consistently to meet new people? They will do the same.

Did you slip into management mode and wonder why your people are waiting around for their one person to do something? Well, they learned it by watching you.

I don't think this is because leaders want to be hypocritical or lazy. I believe the most successful leaders LOVE customers. They want to help customers—it's one of the things that brings them the most joy.

My first encouragement to you is to get back to the place where you are enrolling customers again. You will feel better and your committed team members will start to follow your lead.

My second encouragement to you is that if you feel like you aren't sure who to contact at this point in your career, that is actually to be expected.

There is one very important thing you need to know as a network marketing leader: man cannot live solely on people he knows.

I was leading a coaching group and one of our clients asked a really smart question. She said, "I just moved to a new town and I'm making new friends. I also want to get my business going. How long do I wait before inviting my new friends? I don't want them to think I am being their friend just to sell them something." Great question!

> *There is one very important thing you need to know as a network marketing leader: man cannot live solely on people he knows.*

I shared with her that her problem wasn't when to invite them. It was the fact that her business success was built on the backs of these people, and that's why it didn't feel right. I recommended that she go find some vendor events to showcase her business. This would relieve some pressure on her friendships and she could be much more authentic in her invitation of people she knew.

There are six strategies to connect with people to find out if your products will solve their problems or help them reach their goals. You don't need to pick all of them. Just pick 2-3 total and get really good at them. Choose the ones that bring you the most joy so you will be more motivated to master them.

Strategy #1: People You Know

Most network marketers start with people they know for a few different reasons. First, as they learned about the product, they probably already thought of all the people they knew who would get benefits from the product. Second, there is built-in trust both ways, which makes it a great way to practice without as much judgement. Third, it's how most businesses start. If I were to open a taco restaurant, my first strategy would be to have a grand opening with all of my friends and family.

Most industry training focuses on this strategy only because they are trying to help NEW people be successful, and rightfully so. But what about when you aren't new? You can probably enroll your first 20-30 people through connecting with people you know, but then what? This is why many leaders inadvertently land in management mode. They don't know what to do next. Don't worry, boo, we got you.

Strategy #2: Referrals and Hosts/Hostesses

If your customer doesn't want to build their own business, this doesn't mean they don't want to be involved in spreading the word through the community. Some network marketers prefer to have people host parties/classes/socials or whatever term their company uses. Some prefer to get individual referrals to invite to 1-on-1s. This works well because there are high levels of trust with the endorsement of your customer. Even people who don't buy products from you will often refer others to get something for free. Don't count them out.

Think this way about customers. I care about the customer. The customer cares about their friends/family. Therefore, I care about the customer's friends and family. Have confidence that you are a GIFT to the community. If you don't connect with the community, they might be left interacting with a network marketer who doesn't love people as much as you do. That would be a travesty, so don't wait!

Have confidence that you are a GIFT to the community.

Strategy #3: Vendor Booths or Events

Holiday fairs, farmer's markets, expos, and more. Many venues welcome vendors to bring extra traffic to the event and to keep the event goers happy. People love to shop and tend to be very open-minded. A lot of successful network marketers will make their strategy to sign up for a few of these every month or quarter. This will ensure a steady flow of new connections, signing up of new customers, and scheduling appointments.

When you are at booths, keep a simple set up. Remember what you have already learned about customer overwhelm. More is not better. A clean set up will be more attractive. Stand out in front of the table, smile and use a great pick-up line. Your business will not grow with a shoebox full of raffle entries that you don't want to call, so focus on striking up quality conversations and invite potential customers to appointments or to purchase.

Strategy #4: Networking Events/Speaking

Many businesses join networking groups to make new connections, and this is a great opportunity for you as well. Sometimes these groups will provide opportunities to speak about areas of expertise you have with your product, or in other areas of your life. Either way, this activity creates new connections.

Perhaps you have an area of expertise that compliments your business, and allows speaking opportunities on a separate but still complementary topic. You can work with your networking group to gain more speaking events.

A word of caution for networking events: go for friends, not "contacts." Learn about people's lives and about their problems. Once you know three problems, goals, or needs, it's probably appropriate to offer an appointment. Contribute through leadership of the chapter to build more significant influence.

Strategy #5: Partnering with Business Owners

There are likely many businesses in your area that serve the people you serve, but not in the way you do. This is a great opportunity for partnerships. Network marketers in financial services can partner with various types of agents. Those in health and wellness can partner with health coaches or doctors.

Pick a specific profession and become the "go to" person. Interview 3-5 professionals who you know. Learn their goals, problems, and wants, and then create a customized business overview of how it works in that industry. This will build your confidence, and theirs too!

Strategy #6: Social Media

I met my husband online even before our current social media set up was in existence. I don't think I would have run into him at work, or with friends. I was skeptical that I would find the love of my life online, but didn't have a ton of options. But there he was, and we found each other. Through online dating sites I met so many people that I wouldn't have otherwise met. Going online also led to reconnecting with people I knew. Would you believe that I got matched with my high school prom date?!

Social media platforms can be used to reconnect with people you already know. You can be more proactive using social media to connect with people who have similar interests to you through groups or Instagram to increase the amount of people you know. A third option is to set up a business page and use that to connect with people you don't yet know. Your social media strategy will depend on how long you have been in business, your skills and experience, your resources—like money for advertising—and your preferences.

Why Role-Modeling is Important

> *"A role model in the flesh provides more than inspiration; his or her very existence is confirmation of possibilities one may have every reason to doubt, saying, Yes, someone like me can do this."*

—Sonia Sotomayor

Reason #1: Connecting With Your Team

You don't want to have to start your stories with, "back in my day…" You will likely be met with an eye roll and the network marketing equivalent of "ok boomer." One big question that your team will have is whether or not what you did to be successful STILL works.

You need real, relevant stories. You don't need to be the top enroller on your team, but you need to be dangerous enough to sniff through their BS, and encouraging enough to lift them up. When they are frustrated about three no-shows in a row, you need to be able to respond with, "can I share with you a setback I had last week?" This will normalize the experience and let them know that there is not something wrong with them. As a result, they will be more confident and move into action.

When you are consistently enrolling, you are able to share best practices with your team. At the time I am writing this, social media is all the rage, and in many companies, the top enrollers only operate through social media. But not my client Bailey. Last month she enrolled 32 people, face-to-face. Beast mode. She can share EXACTLY what she is doing today to help her team crack the code and be successful.

When you are consistently enrolling, you are able to share best practices with your team.

Reason #2: It Puts Your Business Back in Your Control

Nothing is more frustrating than feeling powerless about your paycheck, especially if it's important to feed your family. Your team members might only be in their business for a season of their life. Some people might desire the highest ranks but have a LOT of work to do to develop the skills and mindset to be successful. Stress happens when we try to control what we can't control. If we are relying on our team members for our income, this is a recipe for a VERY stressed life.

Give clarity and continue to encourage, train and mentor your team. Just don't wait. It is YOUR job to take care of your family, not theirs. Take control back by enrolling new customers and new builders consistently.

Reason #3: You Haven't Met Some of Your Top People Yet

I want you to look at your spouse, your kids, and some of your best friends. Did you know them in high school? If you are like me, you have a few friends that have known you forever.

I would have been perfectly content marrying my best friend growing up. Chris, if you happen to be reading this, it's not because of some secret crush. It's because I knew him, his family loved me, and we would have built a hockey rink in our backyard. But over the years, my experiences have shaped me into a different version of that kid. As I've grown as a person, moved towns and as my interests have evolved, I have new friends I can't imagine living my life without.

Even today, in theory I'd be perfectly content to never meet another person. But there are people out there who need me as part of their story. And there are people out there who I need as part of mine.

Your entire career won't be built on the first 10 people you met. Don't worry if your "circles" aren't filled in yet. Continuing to enroll gives you space to connect with amazing people.

Reason #4: It's a Great Training Opportunity

Most leaders train their builders using three-way calls. Team members can observe, but they are super attached to the outcome. Are you meeting with a referral? Record the appointment (give the customer something for free in exchange) and you have a great learning opportunity. If you are doing a vendor event, take a new person with you. Let them watch you in action!

Reason #5: It Increases Joy

Leading people is challenging and can be discouraging, especially if it's new to you. Why won't everyone just do what you say? I know, I get it. By continuing to help customers and recruiting new builders, you will still spend at least half of your time getting wins in your business.

You will stay connected to the power of the product so your confidence, enthusiasm, and belief will continue to be contagious.

As a leader, sharing testimonials with your team will continue to build their skill and product conviction. Your positive results with customers will fuel you as you improve your leadership skills, and as your team grows.

Role-modeling isn't about perfection. My definition of role-modeling is to first set a goal. Second, work to reach that goal. Whether you reach that goal or not is irrelevant in role-modeling. The third step is to reflect. Fourth, try again. You are role-modeling character, a customer first mindset, and effort. In order for our team to relate with us, we must actually show them that we AREN'T perfect so they understand they don't have to be perfect to be successful.

> *You are role-modeling character, a customer first mindset, and effort.*

"Customer first" leadership can be summed up by this inspiring quote from Teddy Roosevelt:

> *"It is not the critic who counts; not the man who points out how the strong man stumbles, or where the doer of deeds could have done them better. The credit belongs to the man who is actually in the arena, whose face is marred by dust and sweat and blood; who strives valiantly; who errs, who comes short again and again, because there is no effort without error and shortcoming; but who does actually strive to do the deeds; who knows great enthusiasms, the great devotions; who spends himself in a worthy cause; who at the best knows in the end the triumph of high achievement, and who at the worst, if he fails, at least fails while daring greatly, so that his place shall never be with those cold and timid souls who neither know victory nor defeat."*

This leader, the one in the arena, is one worth following.

121

SECTION 4

EGO LAST

CHAPTER 15

PROVING VALUE V. PROVIDING VALUE

I'll never forget the day I met Jackie. It was a turning point in my life. I would love to tell you it's because I was so eloquent and amazing and my career took off, but it was a different kind of turning point.

I met Jackie through an introduction from my business partner, Karen. They had hit it off and Jackie was interested in 1-on-1 coaching. Jackie has a very large organization, so this fell in the "Tasha" category. I was excited about the call.

Jackie's call started like every potential client call. I gave an agenda. I asked about her goals and challenges. The next answer sent me reeling into a subconscious panic.

Me: "What do you know about me, and the work I do?" (I was expecting a "not much" and I was prepared for that)...

Jackie: "I know that you create Presidential Diamonds." (This is the highest rank in Jackie's company.)

Me: "Uh...ok."

Jackie: "I am very excited to hear whatever brilliance you have to share with me."

On the surface this sounds like an amazing answer. It triggered an insecurity in me and I started fumbling.

I spent the next 30-40 minutes showing off. I don't remember the details, but I imagine there was some statistic throwing and some name dropping.

I talked a lot, and threw out way too many ideas on things we can do to "fix her problems" so she understood that I was in fact, soooo brilliant.

I was SO lucky that Jackie is who she is. She was really excited about the future and we connected with each other really well despite my weirdness. Jackie agreed to start coaching and we set up our next steps.

I ended the Zoom call with a sick feeling in my stomach. The outcomes of that call were perfect, but something felt off.

Then I figured it out. I was trying to PROVE my value instead of PROVIDING value.

Jackie had shared who she thought I was and I was trying to prove to her that it was true. My ego defeated my customer first philosophy that day.

I decided to make a change. I never wanted to think that way again.

Two days later, my former client Daniela and I had a call booked to discuss restarting coaching. I gave her the agenda and asked questions to determine the state of her business for the past six months.

The difference between the calls with Jackie and Daniela was that I had nothing to prove to Daniela. In fact, she was one of the reasons I had the reputation Jackie spoke of. However, it's hard not to feel intimidated around leaders like this. They are just so powerful.

I had made a commitment, though. No more trying to prove myself. After hearing about her business, my next question was, "how can I provide value to you and your family at this stage of your business and life?"

Daniela responded, "I'll take whatever you have." This would have triggered me. It had the same undertones as Jackie's response.

Instead of showing off, I decided to take a different approach. I knew that no matter what level a leader is, they always benefit from reviewing a clear definition of success for the upcoming week. This would allow me to provide some strategies that would be helpful.

However, I wasn't able to help her with this clear definition of success. I couldn't concentrate with all the "dinging" her computer was doing. I could tell she couldn't either, and was starting to get flustered and embarrassed.

I smiled and asked, "are those noises driving you crazy?"

Daniela: "Yes."

Me: "Would you like me to turn all of those off?"

Daniela: "What?!?! You can do that?"

Me: "Yes."

I asked for control over her screen. I took over and conducted a little "tech support." We clicked on the settings and proceeded to turn off all alerts off her computer. There would be no more dinging.

Daniela's eyes softened. Her shoulders relaxed. I explained to her, "you know I read an article that said the 'dinging' activates the same place in your brain as when you hear a lion roar. This dinging during a team meeting, it might be why your whole team is afraid of you." We both laughed.

Then she changed my life with these words, "I don't think you are charging me for this call, but if you were, this would be worth every penny. THANK YOU."

What?

I thought, "this really would have been worth it to you?"

Turning off notifications in theory was a very easy thing for me, but it wasn't easy for her. In that moment, she didn't want a script. She didn't need a strategy. She didn't need me to remind her of her accomplishments.

She needed the dinging to stop so she could think, listen, and make sure her team members weren't distracted during coaching calls or trainings. In my mind, it was a quick google search. But in her mind, I had PROVIDED value.

Show up to provide value, not to prove value.

These two amazing ladies taught me something really important about sales, leadership, and business.

Show up to provide value, not to prove value.

Scenario #1: Explaining a Product

Proving value explains how superior the product is to everything else in the world, explains how it will solve every problem, and includes a detailed scientific description of how the product interacts with parts of your body you didn't know you had.

Providing value gives a super simple explanation that a fourth-grader could understand. The explanation makes the potential customer feel smart. The explanation simply goes over when/how a customer will use the products, and follows up with a "how does that sound?" instead of a "does that make sense?"

Scenario #2: Addressing a Concern

Proving value will hear a concern like, "I could get that at Walmart" and gets defensive. Proving value tells the customer why they are wrong and you are right.

Providing value addresses concerns with a few clarifying questions. When you hear a concern you will seek to understand what they are thinking instead of assuming and trying to convince them.

Scenario #3: Social Proof

Proving value will name drop. There is an arrogant tone that makes people feel bad because other people are doing it and the customer is not part of the cool club.

Providing value will have an encouraging tone. When we are sharing a success story of someone else, it's meant to encourage the potential customer instead of shame them. It sounds more like, "Let me make sure I understand what you are saying... Can I share with you a success story that might be encouraging to you?" Then we tell the story with the intention of being helpful and encouraging instead of using it as a club.

127

Scenario #4: Sharing Personal Success

Proving value will brag with the intention of impressing and receiving more admiration.

Providing value will celebrate with the intention of encouraging people that if "I can do it, you can do it too."

Scenario #5 Solving a Problem

Proving value will show up as Mr./Ms. Fix it or Mr./Ms. Know-it-all, with quick answers that tend to make people feel like they should know the answer. Proving value will give unsolicited advice. People will not want to share their challenges because they won't feel safe or supported.

Proving value will see a problem and check in first. We will ask questions like "are you ok?" or "what have you already tried?" A more humble posture will pause and ask permission to pose a solution. "If I had an idea about that, would that be helpful?" This is respectful and will lead to a much more positive response from your potential customer.

The Temptation of Proving Value

Proving our value to others is a natural part of being human. From when we were young, we intuitively knew how to tease someone to make ourselves feel superior, or to brag, "Look what I did!"

The difference between proving value and providing value is subtle. It's not the activity that gives the "ick factor." It's typically the intention or the posture with which we approach a situation. Proving ourselves occurs when ego takes over, and our insecurities become the driving force of our communication. I know that when I'm feeling out of my league, my ego shows up and only further proves that I am, in fact, out of my league. Yikes!

However, sometimes we try to prove our value because we just don't know any better. Most people around us are constantly trying to prove their value, and we pick up on these habits as we grow up. We want to be the MVP on the sports team, or the top student, so we show off our skills. The adults around us growing up are also trying to prove they belong, and we pick up their habits as well. We also sometimes don't even have the skill to recognize our own posture or know what to do or say to provide true value. I surely don't get it right every day, but I do have a few things that will help you make the shift toward being a true value provider.

First, it helps me to pray. I know the service I provide is an answer to someone's prayers. So if I start my day thinking, "how can I be the answer to someone's prayers today?" I am much more relaxed as I talk to people.

Second, I work hard to increase my own value through personal and professional development. Four of the leaders who I am currently coaching were interested in coaching with me after asking if I knew how to do social media. At the time, I didn't profess to be a "social media expert" like many other coaches did, but I let them know that I knew enough to help them. It turns out what I knew was in fact incredibly helpful! If I had not stayed committed to learning and growing new skills, we all would have missed out on some amazing partnerships.

> *"How can I be the answer to someone's prayers today?"*

Third, I try really hard to ask for agreement before giving advice. Unsolicited advice is often unwelcome, even if you have hired a professional coach whose sole job is to give advice! I will listen and ask, "can I share my opinion with you?" Another good question like this is, "I have a couple of ideas, would you like me to share them with you? Feel free to shoot them down, I'm just brainstorming." I try to make sure to communicate that our conversation is collaborative instead of barking out orders. Now, if only I could practice this habit with my husband!

Fourth, I try to focus on the one person who my message might help. I can't take credit for this life philosophy, I learned this from my client Sheryl. I watched her speak at a workshop and she said, "I am going to tell you a really vulnerable story. But if it helps just one person, it will be worth it." She proceeded to inspire the whole room. Public speaking, whether it is online or from a stage is truly terrifying. There are ALL of those people judging us! But it doesn't matter if they all judge us as long as it changes one person's world.

I am reminded of a story I heard as a young leader. A little boy was walking along the shoreline, and a whole wave of starfish had washed up on shore. He was throwing them back one at a time, clearly not making a dent. A bystander came over and said, "what's the point? You will never get them all. It doesn't matter." The boy responded, "it matters to that one," and threw another one back into the water.

Providing value is about approaching people as though they matter AND we matter. Our ego is going to attempt to muck up our business by trying to take center stage. Remember that our customer and team are center stage. They are the heroes, and we are the guides. Our job is to be the best guides possible so they can feel powerful. Our job is NOT to flex our own power. Committing to providing value is the intention that moves someone from being an icky network marketer to a trusted advisor.

This trust is a great foundation for your growing business.

Customer First Takeaways

• Proving your value and providing value are two different things—don't get them confused.

• It takes a conscious effort not to let our ego take over and try to prove ourselves.

• Work to be the answer to someone's prayers today.

• Increase your own value through personal and professional development so you have more value to give.

• Ask for agreement before giving advice.

• Instead of trying to impress everyone all of the time, remind yourself, "If this helps just one person, I have provided value today.

CHAPTER 16

SOMETIMES IT'S AWKWARD

I remember going to my first big network marketing conference. It was "The Most Powerful Women in Network Marketing," and I was excited.

My friend convinced me to come with her, and then convinced me to get an upgraded ticket to sit with her in the first three rows. The problem was that she had a family emergency, and wasn't able to come. So there I was, sitting in the VIP section but not knowing anyone (and DEFINITELY not feeling very important), and my best seating option was to sit next to two ladies who very clearly were good friends.

Awkward.

How do you handle awkward situations like this? I used to hide and be shy. Or I would fumble around like a dork.

Now I acknowledge the awkwardness. I've learned "awkward" so well that one of my friends actually said that I "embrace the awkward."

"Hi, I'm Tasha. It's nice to meet you. My friend had a family emergency and I don't have anyone to sit with. Can I sit with you?"

"Yes, of course! And would you like to have lunch with us?"

Phew! Awkwardness gone. I've never been really great at small talk, or striking up conversation. I have found most people feel the same way! I used to think that I needed to come up with some super cool pick-up line, and that's what all the successful people in the world did. I have no such gift, if it even exists.

Learning how to acknowledge the awkward has made me, someone who dreads meeting new people, much more confident in almost any situation.

There are so many awkward situations when you are in network marketing.

1. When it feels like asking a certain question is coming out of the blue

2. Doing an appointment and trying to be professional when the person in front of you has known you since you were a baby

3. When a hostess doesn't tell the guests you are going to be showing products

4. Setting up a follow-up time for a decision on buying

5. You haven't followed up with customers in a long time

6. You are new at a networking group

7. You just met someone but think your product will help him or her

What is the best approach in these, and all of the other awkward situations in your business?

The awkward typically comes from the fact that both people involved know it's awkward and don't know how to act. All we need to do is acknowledge the elephant in the room.

We often think that we need to be smooth, perfect, confident, and 100% put together. We think that if we are perfect, people will love us more or value us more.

This makes sense to our brain. Unfortunately, it's not true at all.

One of my favorite quotes is by Angela Lim:

"I saw that you were perfect and I loved you. Then I saw that you were not perfect, and I loved you even more."

It is our vulnerability that makes us endearing and trustworthy, not a perfect ideal we will never attain.

The attempt to look perfect when we are not is not a customer first philosophy. It is an ego first philosophy.

When we put our ego first, we put our customers last. Our ego says, "this is awkward, walk away. Don't show up, you will lose face."

If we listen to this voice, we do nothing. We don't help anyone solve a problem. The customer loses. We lose too.

Research has shown that when we expose a chink in our armor, we actually become MORE trustworthy. Everyone knows there aren't any perfect people in the world. When we attempt to show up as perfect, the person we are communicating with smells BS. They will intuitively start to look for the hole in the argument, or the imperfection.

It is our vulnerability that makes us endearing and trustworthy, not a perfect ideal we will never attain.

However, if you just proactively expose the holes or imperfections, your potential customer will relax and actually defend you.

This is why the "acknowledge the awkward" technique works so well.

You acknowledge the awkward. They tell you it's ok. Both of you feel more comfortable. More trust is built between the two of you. You are in a better position to connect with them on a human level. They are more likely to listen to what you say.

I did this at the beginning of this book. It's awkward that I don't have an active network marketing business. That could be a big detractor for me. If I didn't acknowledge it, you would have likely brought up that objection and invalidated everything I am sharing with you.

But you aren't ignoring me. We have trust built. It's because I just acknowledged the awkward, and explained why it might not be so bad. You likely came up with additional reasons that it would be refreshing to read a book from the customer's perspective instead of from a million-dollar earner. (For the record, I think it's wise to read both types of books to piece your strategy together.)

Let's go through those awkward situations we mentioned earlier, and how we can easily address them so you can move into action instead of be paralyzed with inaction. We are just going to tell them the truth.

When It Feels Like You are Asking a Certain Question Out of the Blue

"This next question might be coming out of the blue, but I want to make sure I personalize this conversation to you, and what you care about. What are the health goals you have for you and your family?"

Doing an Appointment and Trying to Be Professional When the Person in Front of You Has Known You Since You Were a Baby

"I'm a little nervous since we have known each other for a long time. Do you mind if in our appointment, I just treat you as if you are a 'normal customer?' That way you get the best experience possible. Is that fair?"

When a Hostess Doesn't Tell the Guests You are Going to Be Showing Products

"Hi everyone. It looks like you are a little surprised that we are going to be talking about these widgets today. Don't worry, I'm not a crazy salesperson. I'll just ask you a few questions about what's important to you when it comes to _____, walk through why these products might be a good fit for you, and if you want to, I can go over how to buy them so you can get on with your night. How does that sound to everyone?"

Setting up a Follow-up Time For a Decision on Buying

I use this one all the time.

"Ok great, so you are planning on ordering on Friday. I tend to be sort of the anxious type. Will you let me know on Friday when you take care of it? If I don't hear back from you by Saturday I'll reach out. If anything changes for whatever reason, will you let me know? Ok great! Thanks!"

You Haven't Followed Up With Customers in a Long Time

"I know it's been a while since we connected about your _____ products. I'm really sorry about that. I'm calling right now because I'm trying to be better about that. How have you been?"

You are New at a Networking Group

"Hi, I'm new to this networking group and don't know anyone yet. Can you give me a few pointers on how to connect with people here?"

You Just Met Someone and You Think Your Product Will Help Them

"I know I just met you, but I think a product I sell for my work would be helpful to you. Would it be helpful to you if I shared a little about it?"

Acknowledging the awkward is a great way to get out of inaction and into impacting customers. It's the bridge you need to get to learning about them, or your message. Next time you find yourself asking yourself, "This is so awkward because _____. What do I tell them?"

That. Tell them exactly that.

Bonus Tip: Just Because

> *"Just give me a reason, just a little bit's enough. Just a second we are not broken just bent, and we can learn to love again."*
>
> —P!nk

The desire for a reason is at the core of who we are as humans. When we are children we ask, "why?" only to be dismissed by our parents, "just because." If you were like me, the response was, "just because what?!?!" I wanted a reason. Any reason would have been helpful.

A while back I read *The Science of Selling,* and was blown away by a simple thing that helps increase people's responsiveness to your request.

Just give them a reason.

What if by using one word in our communication, we could increase the chances of others taking the action that we want them to take? It's awkward when we don't tell people the reason we want to do something. We need to change that.

In most instances all we need to do to gain agreement is to use the word "because." Yup, that's it. I was blown away.

The research on the word "because" was made famous in what is called "The Copy Machine Study." In the study, a researcher asked people to skip ahead in line to make copies.

In the first trial, the researcher made a request, but didn't give a reason. "Excuse me, I have 5 pages. May I use the Xerox machine?" 60% of people let the researcher skip the line.

> *In most instances all we need to do to gain agreement is to use the word "because."*

In the second trial, the researcher made a request and gave a real reason. ""Excuse me, I have 5 pages. May I use the Xerox machine, because I'm in a rush?" 94% of people complied. That makes sense, until you hear the next trial.

In the third trial, the researcher gave a fake reason. "Excuse me, I have 5 pages. May I use the Xerox machine, because I have to make copies?" 93% of people complied. This is crazy because it's a nonsensical reason. Everyone has to make copies. This study showed that the human mind just needs to have any reason to justify their behavior.

I wanted to take this concept to my toughest "sale," Haley.

At the time I read the study, I could not get Haley to brush her teeth. She was five at the time, and "unadaptable," just like her mom.

We had tried every technique that parents try—rewards, responsibility, guilt, etc.—and nothing worked. As a coach for communicators, this was incredibly frustrating. So I figured there was no loss in trying this "because" theory.

I said, "Okay Haley, please brush your teeth because it will help you to have healthy teeth." And boom, she brushed her teeth.

The second night I tried something different. "Please brush your teeth because it's bedtime." Boom.

The third night I tried a nonsensical reason. "Haley, please brush your teeth because it's time to brush your teeth." She did it.

Interesting. The fourth night I wanted to really test this theory. "Haley, please brush your teeth because the hamper is red."

And no joke…she did it.

I am not proposing you make up nonsensical reasons for your customers or team members to gain agreement. This would be unethical behavior and would violate our customer first philosophy.

However, I do want to challenge you to ensure you're including reasons in your communication.

"Let's set up an appointment" can be adjusted to "let's set up an appointment because it's loud here and I want to pay close attention to what you are saying."

"Put in your credit card" becomes "You will want to put in your credit card and set up your next shipment because running out of product is the worst." (It's true, it is…)

"Are you coming to the team meeting?" shifts to "I hope you come to the team meeting because we will talk about how to invite people. Can you make it?"

The specific formula is [request] because [reason]. Test it out because I think you and the people you speak with will be happier.

See what I did there?

Customer First Takeaways

- If a situation feels a little awkward, just acknowledge the thing that makes it awkward, and gain agreement to continue.

- People aren't looking for perfection—they are looking for people who are genuine.

- Exposing the awkward actually builds credibility instead of diminishing it.

- If you are asking someone to do something, it's awkward not to give them a reason.

Use the word "because" when giving a reason to justify behavior.

CHAPTER 17

I'VE GOT SKILLS, THEY'RE MULTIPLYING

I played basketball in college, but that was a very unlikely outcome for someone like me. Indians are not really known for their athletic prowess.

My grandma had a basketball half-court at her house. Growing up, my mom "made us" go there every weekend, but that's ok, because my uncle would often be there too. He is also a basketball lover. Since we couldn't get by on sheer athletic ability, he taught me the "jumpshot."

Every weekend at my grandma's I would work on jumping, then shooting. It was so hard because I could barely get the ball to the rim as a kid. I would learn to jump, then shoot. It was really difficult for me. I wasn't strong enough at first. But my uncle was my hero, and I wanted him to be proud of me. So I kept shooting. Eventually I got strong enough.

My Sundays practicing with my uncle made me a beast on the Christian Junior High Girls Basketball Circuit. If that doesn't impress you enough, my shooting made me good enough to make the varsity girls basketball team as a freshman in high school. My sophomore year on varsity came and went and I started getting splinters in my bottom from sitting on the bench.

Meanwhile, my softball career was taking off. I was the starting shortstop, and had tons of promise. My sophomore season of basketball ended with virtually no playing time and softball season began the next week.

The truth was, I just wasn't good enough to get playing time. I worked so freaking hard in practice but just wasn't fast enough. I had two choices then. My first choice was to focus on softball. But softball didn't bring me joy like basketball did. My second choice was to improve my basketball skills. I chose the latter.

School started at 7:45am. After school I had practice, and then homework, dinner, and watching the Lakers. In the evening there were too many cars driving up and down the street to practice, so 6:00am it was. I woke up early, grabbed a ball and did ball-handling drills for 30 minutes at least three mornings a week. I practiced my footwork and my muscle memory. I knew I couldn't be the fastest, but I could be the smartest and quickest with my hands.

When I broke my right middle finger (yes, you read that right, and it was as funny as you think) playing softball, I focused on the skill of shooting and dribbling left-handed.

While I could never get fast enough (or tall enough) to have the most shots on my team, I knew that when I DID have an opportunity, I would never miss or lose the ball because I had perfected the skills!

I'm happy to report that my junior and senior years of high school I rarely left the court, and was able to make the basketball team at UC San Diego. Skills really do matter.

Action is important. Natural talent is nice. But underdogs can win at most things because we can always get better at skills.

It's likely you are reading this book because you are hoping to achieve professional levels of income. I learned really early in my direct sales career that if you want to earn income like a professional, you need to act like one. This made sense to me. My dad is a doctor. I know how much school he went to. I have seen all his huge books at the office. I know he goes to conferences to learn more. I also knew how much he made.

What are skills?

A skill is a <u>learned</u> power of doing something <u>competently</u>.

Actions + skills = results.

I am addressing skills in the ego section because our ego keeps us from learning the skills we need to. Let's look at my basketball example for a moment. I could have said, "my coach is dumb, I never miss a shot. I should be playing." I had to suspend my ego and acknowledge I wasn't fast enough. I could have waited for my right hand to heal and taken the spring off. That would have made sense to everyone. I had to be willing to look foolish shooting left-handed until my muscle memory was built.

> *Actions + skills = results.*

There are two categories of skills in network marketing. For now, I want you to focus on the top five sales skills, and then the top five leadership skills.

Sales Skills

Time Management/Planning

Do you do what you say you are going to do? Do you have a plan for each week? Do you stay focused on your priorities?

Setting Appointments

When you offer people appointments, do they schedule with you?

Closing

Do at least half of customers buy on the first appointment?

Is the average order at least 100-product value?

Lead Generation

Are you able to consistently gain new contacts through referrals, hosting group events, networking, speaking, vendor booths, social media, etc.? "I can do this" means you are able to generate enough new "leads" each month to reach your enrollment goals.

Customer Retention

Are people reordering the following month and beyond? Are you in consistent connection with your customers?

Leadership Skills

Recruiting and Launching Team Members

How many new team members have you "launched" in the past three months? I define a launch as someone who enrolls his or her first customer.

Communicating Vision

Do I have a vision that I'm excited about? Do the people on my team know what they are a part of?

Do I interrupt with answers? Do I understand the core issue holding my team member back? Could I summarize if I wanted to?

Listening and Gaining Agreement

Are you on the same page with your customers and team members? Are people engaged with you, or do they think you are kind of bossy or annoying? When you go somewhere, do they generally agree to go with you?

Positive Team Culture

Do I have a team culture that is vibrant, exciting, and the place to be? Does our team culture reflect my vision/idea of success for my business?

How to Improve Skills

Building skills starts with knowing what the skills are. I am typically met by a range of emotions when explaining these skills. It starts with an "oh crap I'm screwed" and quickly turns to hope when it clicks into

"Where there is a skill, there is a way"

- Cassie Stutzman.

Step 1: Define the Skills and What Success Looks Like

We have just made a list of skills to focus on for your professional development. We also have an idea of the difference between good and poor results. You can now focus on one or two of the skills at a time.

Step 2: Give Yourself a Rating

There are four skill levels when you are learning something new. Rating them will take your emotions out of your skill development process and help you to be encouraged by your progress over time.

Skill level 0 = I have never done this before. This is exciting! There is only one way to go from here! Up!

Skill level 1 = I am just starting to learn this skill. I am making attempts but I am not good, yet. I try, but I still kind of stink at this one.

Skill level 2 = I can do this and get predictable, positive results.

Skill level 3 = I am a rockstar.

It takes a lot of humility to acknowledge you excel in one skill but are still developing another. And this is where many people get stuck. It's impossible to skip the part where you aren't yet an expert.

There aren't any shortcuts (other than gaining wisdom) to skill level 3. I often have to remind myself when I'm starting something new that the only way out is THROUGH. If it's hard at first, don't be discouraged. There is an African proverb that states, "Smooth seas do not make skillful sailors."

Redo your ratings every three months and celebrate the success of your focused effort on skill development.

Step 3: Seek Wisdom

What got you here won't get you there. This goes for strategy, action, and also wisdom. The wisdom I currently have is enough to get me to this point, right here. But if I want to go somewhere else, I will likely need someone else's wisdom.

Choose one or two skills you are going to develop, and focus your professional development in this area only. This strategy will allow you to get traction quickly in your business. Professional development

What got you here won't get you there.

can be very overwhelming if you try to listen to everything and apply it all at the same time.

If your skill focus is closing, make sure the books you are reading and courses you are taking are on closing. If I wanted to get really good at baking so I could wow my family next Christmas, I wouldn't attend a cooking class on Chinese food. Do not let a fear of missing out lead you to overwhelming yourself with learning you won't be able to apply.

Step 4: Create and Practice the Process

Once you learn how to execute a skill, put it in writing so it creates predictable results, and so you don't slide backwards in skill level. This will keep you from missing items or making unnecessary mistakes. If you are having a bad day, your outline will make it easier to be successful even when your brain isn't fully functioning. When you create the process, your customers, team and bank account will thank you.

As you get started with your process, don't forget to practice. It will be really nerve-wracking if you practice for the first time on real people.

You can practice with a team member. You can practice with your spouse. You can practice with a stuffed animal. Just do a couple of run-throughs and your skill will be higher when you are actually with a person.

Step 5: Get Out in the "Real World"

You don't have a skill until you prove it in the real world. Real world experience builds skills more than anything else.

Real world experience builds skills more than anything else.

Step 6: Reflect and Adjust

Skills are born through learning, practice, experience, and reflection. I might find that I have a sales conversation outline, but I keep botching the close. Maybe it doesn't feel like me. Maybe it's wrong. I will likely need to revisit my training or ask questions to someone with more experience than me in order to adjust and get the results I want.

Customer First Takeaways

- Just wanting to be successful isn't enough.

- To improve results, increase action and increase skills.

- The major sales skills are: time management, setting appointments, closing, lead generation, and customer retention.

- The major leadership skills are: recruiting and launching new builders, communication vision, coaching team members, listening and gaining agreement, and creating positive team culture.

- To improve skills: define success, rate yourself, seek wisdom, make a process, get out in the "real world," reflect and adjust.

CHAPTER 18

SEEK TO UNDERSTAND FIRST

The other day I worked with a client on an outline for recruiting business owners. At the end, she asked, "What do I say if they want to think about it?"

I'm sure you have had similar questions about what to say to someone. Often, we actually have the wrong question. Often, it's not about what you need to tell them—it's about what you need to *ask* them.

People love to be guided and cared for, but they do not want to simply be told what to do. Human nature is to resist "know-it-alls." Think about all the fights spouses get into because "you just aren't listening to me!" or "I don't need you to fix this right now!" Or maybe it's just me...

As humans, we want to be seen, heard, and we want to know our opinions matter. We feel this way, and so do our customers and our team members.

> *Often, it's not about what you need to tell them—it's about what you need to ask them.*

We need to fight the temptation for our ego to boss everyone around. Taking the time to truly understand customers will put them first.

The problem with the "think about it" objection my client mentioned earlier is that we don't have enough information to help customers with their decision. It could be that they are simply processing, it could be that they want to research something you said, or they might not even know what they need to think about and it was a knee jerk response.

Addressing Concerns

I am going to lay out the process in "addressing concerns." When someone gives us a concern (customer or team member) our ego wants to quickly provide a solution to the concern. We need to do better than that.

Most people skip right to "providing a solution" without any of the listening. This leads to arguments and frustration on both sides. The process I am about to outline works with customers, team members, and conversations in your "regular" life. I have taught my daughters this process to avoid fights and negotiate their playtime.

Step 1: Seek to Understand

We have already laid the groundwork for trust when we gained input initially. We seek to understand when we ask someone about their goals or problems. We seek to understand when we ask what is important to them, or how something will impact their overall quality of life.

We seek to understand when someone gives a concern. Many people struggle with good listening because they don't know how to do it.

My favorite questions are:

1. Tell me more
2. What do you mean by that?
3. What else?

Step 2: Summarize

One of my previous leaders said to me once, "there are three sides to every story. What they think happened, what you think happened, and what actually happened." That always stood out to me.

There is a big difference between what we think they mean and what they actually mean. An important step in gaining agreement is to summarize or restate what they said, just to make sure you understand.

I usually like to just say, "Let me make sure I understood what you just said… is there anything I missed?"

It doesn't matter if you are right or wrong. If you are right, they will feel heard. If you are wrong, they will correct you and they will feel heard.

Either way, trust is built.

Step 3: If… then…

This is the star. This the gaining agreement question where we pause and ask for permission to give advice. I was once asked, "Can I give you advice?" I said, "sure." She responded, "Don't ever give advice without permission." Point taken.

How you ask the agreement question is going to vary based on the situation, but here are some examples:

1. If I shared a few other options that might be in your price range, would that be helpful?

2. If we did this call over webcam, would that make it easier for you to attend because you don't have childcare?

3. If I shared my outline with you, would that be helpful?

The trick here is to actually care about their answers. One obstacle we discussed earlier is that we are attached to the outcome. The gaining agreement question could be manipulative if you use it for evil and not good. Ask the question. "If I shared a few other options that might be in your price range, would that be helpful?" and wait for their answer.

"Don't ever give advice without permission."

Just today, I got a friend request from a network marketer. I confirmed the company that we were connected through, and then asked, "If I sent you a few YouTube videos that are specific to your company, would that be helpful?" She responded, "no thank you." Wait, what? Ouch.

My ego said, "Do you know who you are talking to?" and "why did you friend request me if you don't love my brilliant training?" But that's not helpful, is it? I asked the question. I meant it. I needed to be ok with the answer. I stepped away from my messages bewildered, but in the meantime she asked me another question. Go figure.

For what it's worth, the correct answer to a "no thank you" is "well if you ever change your mind, you know where to find me."

Step 4: Provide a Solution

Once they agree to hearing a solution, you have bypassed your ego and now can help your customer or team member in a way that makes them feel valued and cared for. Customer first network marketing doesn't mean being a pushover for any concern. It doesn't mean walking away and saying, "aw shucks, they couldn't afford it so I'll put the customer first and walk away."

They said they can't afford it, not "go to hell I hate you." It is our obligation as a customer first network marketer to understand, summarize, and offer to find a solution.

Now is the time to pose a couple of options that might work for them.

Step 5: Get Their Opinion on a Solution

Once you offer a couple of solutions, it's time to gain agreement once again. I like to use questions like:

1. How does that sound?
2. How does that feel?
3. What do you think about that?
4. Does that work better for you?

Again, we need to actually listen to their response. The "how does that sound?" is not simply to get an affirmative answer. We actually care. Say it slowly, look them in the eyes and work WITH them.

A Few Thoughts on Listening

There is a big difference between listening and hearing. Hearing is just what your ears do. Listening is about paying attention to the essence of the words, and allowing space for the other person to express themselves. Listening is about seeking to understand what the other person is saying.

I know 100% we have it in us to be good at listening even if we feel like we aren't. In my job as a business coach, I HAVE to listen. If I don't listen well to my clients, I will alienate them and prescribe the wrong strategy. This will kill my business and I'll be back at my corporate job. I listen like my livelihood depends on it.

There is a big difference between listening and hearing.

Things are different with Charlie though. He is legally required to stay with me. I know without a doubt that he loves me and it's much harder to go date than to stay married to me. I don't take him for granted and I very much appreciate him. He is pretty hot, supports my dreams (even when it's super risky), and brings me tacos whenever I want. But since Charlie loves me unconditionally, I am often a sloppy listener.

This is horrible because a quick answer makes him feel inadequate. I often don't know if he wants a solution or just to vent. And he really resists being told what to do. I'm pretty sure if I did that to my clients, they would feel the same way.

So what solves listening problems?

First, better questions help. Not all questions are created equal. "Are you interested in X product?" doesn't lend itself to listening as much as, "What is important to you when it comes to Y type of product?"

The second thing that will solve listening problems in your business is more lead generation. Attachment to the outcome creates stress. Stress forces us back to previous habits, which include poor listening and fixing problems. We get more attached to outcomes when we don't have options. For example, if you have one appointment a week, you are more attached to whether or not they buy. This one person defines if you are successful or not. You can't control this, which puts you into stress.

However, if you have been proactively creating more contacts, you have five appointments that week. If the first person doesn't enroll, no problem. You have four more. Since you are unattached to the outcome, you are able to be a better listener AND are likely to get better results.

The same works for your team members. It's easier to listen to them when you have recruiting appointments scheduled. You know that whatever happens is going to be ok because you are controlling what you can control: your activity.

I have a list of "oh crap" questions taped to my monitor. I learned these in the book, *The Coaching Habit*. They ground me when I don't know what to do with a difficult situation.

1. What's on your mind?
2. And what else?
3. What's the real challenge here?
4. What do you want?
5. How can I help?
6. If you are saying yes to this, what you are saying no to?
7. What was most useful for you?

I continually keep my ear out for great questions and keep them handy so I can be a better listener. What's really cool is that as I become a better listener, I get better results, and then I get less attached to the outcome.

Customer First Takeaways

- Our ego wants to be right, not be collaborative.

- Listen first, then work with the other person to come up with a solution.

- Better listening comes from being unattached and asking better questions.

CHAPTER 19

YOU ARE THE REAL DEAL

Can you believe this message I got?

"Tasha, you are totally a fraud. I know the truth and everyone is going to find out you are just making this stuff up as you go. I know that you don't actually know what you are doing. Yes, you are crushing it now, but it's likely short-lived and I don't think you are ever going to sell anything again."

Ouch. I got messages like this between every coaching call during the "best time of my professional life." I got them every morning when I woke up, before I went to sleep. Sometimes I would get these messages in the middle of the night. They would wake me up and I couldn't fall back asleep. Putting yourself out there in the world is really hard, especially when you are literally selling yourself.

This kind of criticism wasn't new to me. I have had to encounter it at every turn. I've talked about basketball and hockey in this book, but my best sport is actually softball. My freshman year of high school I beat out a senior starter for the starting shortstop position.

I was recognized with all-league honors at the age of 13. There were high hopes for my future as coaches casually talked about college and the fact that I threw as hard as an Olympian. As soon as this kind of recognition started, so did the criticism.

"Don't screw this up."

"Oh look, I knew you couldn't do it again."

It was unfortunate, but since it was just softball, the effects on my life were low. Basketball was above and beyond my favorite sport anyway.

This criticism was different because this is my sales training company. THIS is my dream. I believe this is my calling and I took it very seriously. On the outside I would smile, tell jokes, and look clients straight in the eye and tell them they could accomplish anything.

However, the criticism was literally killing me. The stress was so fierce it caused massive overwhelm under the hoodie. I became so paranoid that I got a dark purple rash like it was something out of an X-Men movie. It covered my neck and chest. I couldn't sleep for more than two hours without taking swigs of NyQuil. I had to take some horrible medicine to try to calm the itching but the side effect was…paranoia. So it just got worse. I only had to go to the ER once…but only because my dad is a doctor and had supplies available to me.

Can you believe someone can be so mean? I'm sure you have already guessed the punchline.

That "someone" criticizing and attacking me was…me.

Hi, I'm Tasha and I have impostor syndrome. At the time of this writing, it has been 11 days since my last "episode." As I write these last several pages, my chest is itchy again since being at the end here means that someone (you) is actually going to read this. I really hope you don't think I'm a fraud. Can you relate to this feeling?

Impostor syndrome is this feeling like you are doing well right now, but that someone is going to find out that you are a fraud and that you don't know what you are doing.

My coach diagnosed me with "impostor syndrome." She said the number one symptom I was having was that the more success I had, the more I felt it was undeserved. Umm…thanks coach, I'm not sure that's very encouraging. It did help to have a name for it, but I still didn't really know what caused it.

Then I found a book called *The Leading Brain*. I'm a bit of a neuroscience and behavioral psychology nerd and I love finding new ways to hack our minds to improve performance. I'm hoping you have figured out that's one of my obsessions by now. It opened my eyes to what often causes impostor syndrome and gave me some actions to overcome it and kick it to the curb. Then I started healing, and if any of this resonates with you, you are on your way to healing too!

The first thing in the book to strike me was to learn that the most common type of people who suffer from impostor syndrome are highly motivated overachievers who have expert intuition.

Here is how it works. Motivated high achiever gets to work. They develop what is called "unconscious competence" where they are really good at what they do, but they don't know how they do it. It's literally ingrained in their being through a combination of talent, skills, and experience. They start to develop expert intuition where their gut starts working better than their head.

Well, the expert intuition leads to amazing results, but the achiever doesn't know how they did it! The results then get chalked up to luck. In my case, I added in a little, "I'm making this up." I neglected the MBA, the 17 years of sales and leadership experience, countless seminars and dozens of books. I wasn't making it up, but it FELT like I was.

> *The most common type of people who suffer from impostor syndrome are highly motivated overachievers who have expert intuition*

Unfortunately, since I am a human, my feelings were my reality.

The worst part about this was that I knew my thinking was off. Instead of only suffering from impostor syndrome, I also heaped a whole bunch of shame on it. I had a battle in my mind. It started with, "you aren't ever going to sell anything again" and then I added, "you are so stupid for thinking you aren't going to sell anything again."

You can imagine how unhelpful that thinking was. The market was going to test me enough. The work was challenging enough. I didn't need to spend all of that time adding to the challenges.

It doesn't matter if you struggle with impostor syndrome or not. If you do, this next part is for you. If you don't, someone you care about does, and this next part is for you. We cannot put customers first with impostor syndrome at the helm.

Let's talk about how to work through this so you can show up for your customers, your team, and your loved ones. But most importantly, let's talk about how to work through this so you can show up for yourself.

Big Idea #1: It's Normal

It's been said that at some point in their lives, 60% of people experience impostor syndrome. I didn't even know it existed. If I would have known that this caused my eventual poor softball performance, I would have been able to correct it. Who knows what could have happened? Maybe I would have just attributed my sophomore year to impostor syndrome, gotten back up and thrived. Instead, perhaps I believed the impostor syndrome and switched sports to basketball, where I was more comfortable as an underdog.

Big Idea #2: Acknowledge Your Imperfections

God doesn't make perfect people. We all have flaws and imperfections. If you are like me, you might dismiss recognition by thinking, "well you don't actually know how imperfect I am."

So what? What is your actual point? We are all imperfect. AND we all have things we are awesome at. Having imperfections doesn't make you less qualified on the things you are good at. It just means that you are human.

I'm sure it's shocking for you to hear me admit that I am, in fact, not perfect. I am not always the best listener and I do have a tendency to rush to fixing problems that don't need to be fixed. My unbridled optimism can make me blind to flaws in my strategy. And God help everyone if I'm "hangry." I need to just accept that I'm imperfect before I can move forward.

Big Idea #3: Deconstruct Success

As high achievers, we spend a lot of time focusing on what we did wrong when we don't reach a goal. But have you ever noticed when you do reach a goal, it's a quick high-five to yourself and then you are on to the next goal?

What if we spent more time studying what made us successful, instead of all of our time studying what made us miss the mark? Whatever we focus on grows.

I coached a leader a few years ago who is incredibly successful. Her leaders asked her, "what have you done to be successful?" She had just celebrated unprecedented success. She said, "nothing, I just have good people."

I called BS on her. Instead of accepting that remark, I asked her, "What did you do as a leader that contributed to that success?" We made a list. She is constantly inviting people to build the business. She had really well-functioning group coaching programs that she had built over a span of four years. She rocked her in-person events. And she wisely had me train her team on their sales and recruiting processes. ;) Those were not things everyone was doing.

> **Whatever we focus on grows.**

When she became aware of the things she was doing to be successful, her confidence soared. In addition, she could give better mentorship to her new leaders. Leading became easier for her because now she could repeat those behaviors to create more success!

When you win, take five minutes to ask yourself, "what did you do as a leader to create this success?" Being aware of what created success will build your confidence.

Big Idea #4: Stand Firm in Your Leadership Superpower

"Compare and despair" is a deadly toxin to your life and your business. I compare myself to other coaches all of the time. "Wow, her energy is so infectious, I wish I had that kind of enthusiasm." "He has SO many friends and connections—I'll never be able to have that." Can you relate?

Many of us strive to be "more like THAT leader." In theory, this makes sense because "that leader" is more successful than we are. The problem with this professional development approach is that it is just 100% wrong.

Gallup's research shows that people want four things from their leader: trust, compassion, stability, and hope. Followers don't care how you deliver it. We all have the ability to deliver these to the people we lead.

"Compare and despair" is a deadly toxin to your life and your business.

I have studied so many top performers, looking for the pattern so I could bottle it, and sell it. I'm sorry to report that there isn't a true pattern of what exactly they do or what they say. But there IS a pattern. They spend most of their time leaning into their leadership superpower.

Your leadership superpower is YOUR unique combination of how YOU provide trust, compassion, stability, and hope. Each successful leader I have worked with is different. One loves new things, and has built her fortune opening countries for her company. Another leader loves to meet new people, and befriends every soccer mom in her town on the weekends. A third leader rallies her team around every contest imaginable,

Your leadership superpower is YOUR unique combination of how YOU provide trust, compassion, stability, and hope.

because she loves to see them win. A fourth leader can move the world through doing Facebook lives.

They are all different in their strategy but they all deliver the same things to their customers and team: trust, compassion, stability, and hope.

Stop asking, "should I be doing what they are doing?" Any question that starts with "should" is likely the wrong question.

Ask the following questions instead:

- How can I be more trustworthy?
- How can I show more compassion?

- How can I show stability for my team?
- How can I inspire hope for others?

If you are reading this chapter, you are already off to a great start! You have learned how to explain the agenda of an appointment to increase trust. You have learned different questions to ask a customer to show that you care about him or her. You have committed to leading by example, which shows stability. You have worked hard to create processes to empower and give hope to your customers and team.

As you continue to ask yourself, "what did I do to create this success?" you will see a pattern emerge. Take note of which actions create trust, compassion, stability, and hope.

If you want some help with this, I have a specific checklist you can follow to learn your superpower at customerfirstbook.com/superpower.

Download a checklist you can follow to learn your superpower at customerfirstbook.com/ superpower

Big Idea #5: Have a Support System

It has been said, "encouragement is oxygen to the soul." Surround yourself with people who will tell impostor syndrome to hit the road. I used to struggle in private and self-talk myself into the abyss. However, I have found it a lot healthier to send an SOS text to the people whose job it is to help me win. I've learned to "talk about my feelings." I will text my coach when I'm doubting myself. I will talk to my business partner (who, thank God, has a counseling degree). Now that I know what impostor syndrome is, I can give it a name.

Me: I'm struggling right now. I feel like an impostor.

Support system: Get your S#$% together. You are a F#$*& winner.

Support system: Here are 3 texts about how much you help people. (I get screenshots)

Me: Ok thanks. Bye.

It's also super important not only to have friends that support you, but strong mentoring and coaching.

Mentoring is someone who informally guides you. A coach is someone you hire to make sure you are set up to win. Mentors and coaches will help you improve your skills and mindset to improve your results over and over. You will be able to continue to bolster your confidence by getting help with any skill gaps you have.

Big idea #6: Believe the People Who Believe in You

There are a lot of really smart people who believe in me and my abilities. I'm guessing that's the same for you. I used to spend a lot of mental energy telling them they were wrong. But…wait a second. They are super successful, and in any other situation I would trust their judgement. So why would this time be any different?

Sometimes (ok, all the time) I get intimidated by some of my clients. They are the titans in their respective fields. Who am I to lead THEM? Well, they chose me. And maybe…they are right!

Do you have people in your life who you respect? Do they believe in you? Stop fighting them. Just borrow their belief and move forward. They aren't wrong unless you decide you want to prove them wrong. And why would you do that?

Big Idea #7: Actually Celebrate

My favorite quote of all time is from Marianne Williamson.

> "Our deepest fear is not that we are inadequate. Our deepest fear is that we are powerful beyond measure. It is our light, not our darkness that most frightens us. We ask ourselves, 'Who am I to be brilliant, gorgeous, talented, fabulous?' Actually, who are you not to be? You are a child of God. Your playing small does not serve the world. There is nothing enlightened about shrinking so that other people won't feel insecure around you. We are all meant

159

to shine as children do. We were born to make manifest the glory of God that is within us. It's not just in some of us; it's in everyone. And as we let our own light shine, we unconsciously give other people permission to do the same. As we are liberated from our own fear, our presence automatically liberates others."

Friend, celebrate your shine. Every time one of my kids gets a new belt we tell him or her we are proud of him or her and take him or her out to dinner. We celebrate them! Celebrate yourself the same way you would celebrate your family or your team members. Your celebration will inspire others to celebrate as well. Then life will be one big party.

Customer First Takeaways

- If you feel like an impostor sometimes, it's normal.

- We are our own worst enemy but we can engage with these feelings instead of ignoring them.

- Acknowledge your imperfections, deconstruct success, stand firm in your superpower, have a support system and believe them.

- When you win, CELEBRATE.

Show up, and shine. Your customers and team need something only you can provide, because you are the only "you" out there.

CHAPTER 20

AND THEN, THERE WAS JOY.

Think back to why you decided to start your business.

For me, I was done with salary caps, driving two hours a day, and feeling like I wasn't making enough of an impact with my life. I wanted less time in a cage.

I wanted more time with my family, more time to be creative, and more time to live my purpose.

I wanted more joy. I'm thinking that if you drill down to the core of your "why," you want more joy too. I could spend months teaching you wording, strategies, and skills. But NONE of that matters if I don't teach you how to have joy.

Joy comes from customers first, team second, and ego third.

Impacting customers creates joy.

Significance of helping builders and creating a team creates joy.

Joy is waiting for you in your business.

Our ego prevents us from feeling true joy.

We are all ultimately searching for more joy in our lives. As our journey together in this book comes to a close, I want to encourage you that JOY IS WAITING FOR YOU IN YOUR BUSINESS.

You may be wondering if joy is even possible. When I met my client Robbie, I told her I would help her get her joy back. She flatly responded, "impossible." Thankfully, through the steps you have read in this book, I was able to prove her wrong and now she shows up with a joy beam coming out of her like a Care Bear.

Like all good things in life, we must work for joy. We need to be proactive about creating joy. It won't fall in our lap. What's strange about seeking joy, though, is that the work is not toilsome or frustrating. We aren't afraid of hard work—we just want to make sure our hard work matters.

So how do you do work that matters?

Be PROUD of what you do. Seek EXCELLENCE, not perfection. Run your business with true INTEGRITY. Improve your SKILLS. Be KIND to yourself.

And if you are in a sales business, for goodness sake, actually learn how to sell.

RESOURCES

Templates and Downloads

Download a cheat sheet to "The 5 Keys to Make the Sales Process Enjoyable to You and Your Customer"

Customerfirstbook.com/keys

Download a template to use for your "Training Manual"

Customerfirstbook.com/training

Complete a network marketing skills assessment

Customerfirstbook.com/skills

Download a checklist with instructions to determine your unique "Leadership Superpower"

Customerfirstbook.com/superpower

1-on-1 Coaching

As a leader, we know that you are always pouring into other people. Who is pouring into you? If no one is pouring into you, it's easy for your cup to run empty. The #1 best decision I made in my business was to start it. The next best decision was to hire Heather, whose job it is to help me win. For me, I didn't want to have to learn through the school of hard knocks. I wanted to go faster.

If speed is important to you, I recommend that you find an experienced coach to encourage you, support your skill development, and help you with clarity.

1-on-1 coaching does NOT have to be out of reach. We have coaching programs for those just starting out, and for those with large organizations. Go to emergesalestraining.com/private to learn more and connect with us.

Group Coaching and Online Courses

The Emerge Surge is a membership group for our tribe of network marketers committed to changing people's lives. Inside the Emerge Surge you will quickly learn how to get more sales, empower your team, become a confident recruiter, and grow your business through social media.

Inside the Surge, you will discover basic and advanced training around sales, recruiting, leadership and social media that you can work through at your own pace. You will also have access to live and recorded weekly calls and a coaching team ready to answer your questions, encourage you, and help push you forward.

Learn more at emergesalestraining.com/emergesurge.

Speaking Events, Podcasts, and Webinars

Tasha and her team are available to serve and add value to YOUR team. Depending on availability and the size of your team, we would love to be able to share the Customer First message, or help your team with any other training needs.

Go to emergesalestraining.com/speak to connect with us.

Resources Referenced in Customer First

Fabritius, Friederike, and Hans Werner Hagemann. *The Leading Brain: Neuroscience Hacks to Work Smarter, Better, Happier.* TarcherPerigee, 2018.

Hoffeld, David. *The Science of Selling: Proven Strategies to Make Your Pitch, Influence Decisions, and Close the Deal.* TarcherPerigee, 2016.

Pink, Daniel H. *Drive: the Surprising Truth about What Motivates Us.* Canongate Books, 2018.

Rath, Tom, and Barry Conchie. *Strengths Based Leadership: Great Leaders, Teams, and Why People Follow.* Gallup Press, 2008.

Stanier, Michael Bungay. *The Coaching Habit Say Less, Ask More & Change the Way You Lead Forever.* Box of Crayons Press, 2016.

The Copy Machine Study:

https://jamesclear.com/copy-machine-study

Connect With Us

Free Facebook Groups:

Emerge Sales Rock Stars:

https://www.facebook.com/groups/EmergeSalesTrainingRockStars/

The Christian Network Marketer's Community:

https://www.facebook.com/groups/cnmcommunity/

The Sales Journey for Network Marketers Podcast
- iTunes
- Google Play
- Stitcher

Facebook

@emergesalestraining

Instagram

@emergesalestraining

@tashasmith15

Youtube

youtube.com/tashasmith15

Email success stories: team@emergesalestraining.com

Tasha's Favorite Quotes

"Life is a daring adventure or nothing."

—Helen Keller

"People don't care how much you know until they know how much you care."

—Teddy Roosevelt

"The purpose of business is to create and keep a customer."

—Peter Drucker

"Our deepest fear is not that we are inadequate. Our deepest fear is that we are powerful beyond measure. It is our light, not our darkness that most frightens us. We ask ourselves, 'Who am I to be brilliant, gorgeous, talented, fabulous?' Actually, who are you not to be? You are a child of God. Your playing small does not serve the world. There is nothing enlightened about shrinking so that other people won't feel insecure around you. We are all meant to shine as children do. We were born to make manifest the glory of God that is within us. It's not just in some of us; it's in everyone. And as we let our own light shine, we unconsciously give other people permission to do the same. As we are liberated from our own fear, our presence automatically liberates others."

—Marianne Williamson

"Encouragement is oxygen to the soul."

—Anonymous

"I saw that you were perfect and I loved you. I saw that you were not perfect and I loved you more."

—Angela Lim

Made in the USA
Coppell, TX
21 February 2020